WAINWRIGHT'S
DESTRUCTIBLE
COLOURABLE
FLASHCARDABLE
DOODLE QUOTATION GUIDE
TO
A CHRISTMAS CAROL
BY
CHARLES DICKENS

QUOTATIONS CHOSEN AND DRAWN BY EDWARD WAINWRIGHT

ISBN: 9781082129254

How to Abuse This Very Precious Book

THIS BOOK IS MEANT TO HELP YOU TO REMEMBER USEFUL QUOTATIONS SO THAT YOU CAN USE THEM IN YOUR EXAM. TO DO THAT YOU CAN ABUSE THIS BOOK HOWEVER YOU LIKE — BUT

HERE ARE SOME IDEAS:

1. WHERE THERE ARE ALREADY DOODLES, COLOUR THEM IN— IT'S A RELAXING THING TO DO WHEN YOU'VE NO BRAIN LEFT FOR OTHER REVISION.

2. WHERE THERE ARE QUOTATIONS WITH NO DOODLE, DOODLE YOUR OWN DOODLE TO SUIT IT. DOODLE.

3. IF YOU THINK A QUOTATION IS VERY IMPORTANT, TEAR IT OUT OF THE BOOK AND STICK IT UP SOMEWHERE YOU'LL SEE IT OFTEN. SCATTER THEM AROUND THE HOUSE TO DELIGHT YOUR FAMILY.

4. SHARE YOUR BEAUTIFUL OR HILARIOUS DOODLES ONLINE— YOUR FRIENDS NEED THEM!

Can't draw? Don't worry!

There are some memorably terrible doodles in here — the important part is that they're memorable and help you to learn the quotations.

Draw, colour, share with your friends.

(And please, please don't laugh at my sheep.)

One more thing (or three):

Don't forget to use your copy of "A Christmas Carol" with this book. Also, use a dictionary or the internet to look up unfamiliar words and when you've done that label them, or they'll be in your mental sepulchre forever.

Finally, if it's not a character talking, the words probably belong to the omniscient narrator.

Stave One: Marley's Ghost

STAVE ONE TIMELINE

Marley is dead.

Scrooge is described.

Scrooge is horrible to Fred.

"Marley was dead."

FLASHCARD

TEAR THIS PAGE OUT, FILL THIS SIDE IN AND BINGO! YOU HAVE A FABULOUS FLASHCARD.

THIS QUOTATION IS FROM STAVE __1__ .

THE WORDS BELONG TO _____

_____ .

ONE LITERARY TECHNIQUE USED IS

Simily .

ANOTHER LITERARY TECHNIQUE USED IS

_____ .

THE WORD CLASS OF THE KEY WORD

" _____ " IS _____ .

WRITE THE QUOTATION HERE — MAKE SURE IT IS <u>EXACTLY</u> THE SAME AS IT IS ON THE OTHER SIDE!

ASK: HOW DOES THIS MAKE YOU FEEL?

ASK: WOULD VICTORIANS HAVE FELT THE SAME?

ASK: HOW DOES THIS LINK TO CONTEXT?

ASK: DO OTHER QUOTATIONS LINK TO THIS?

"Old Marley was as dead as a doornail."

FLASHCARD

TEAR THIS PAGE OUT, FILL THIS SIDE IN AND BINGO! YOU HAVE A FABULOUS FLASHCARD.

THIS QUOTATION IS FROM STAVE _____.

THE WORDS BELONG TO _____

_____.

ONE LITERARY TECHNIQUE USED IS

_____.

ANOTHER LITERARY TECHNIQUE USED IS

_____.

THE WORD CLASS OF THE KEY WORD

" _____ " IS _____.

WRITE THE QUOTATION HERE — MAKE SURE IT IS <u>EXACTLY</u> THE SAME AS IT IS ON THE OTHER SIDE!

ASK: HOW DOES THIS MAKE YOU FEEL?

ASK: WOULD VICTORIANS HAVE FELT THE SAME?

ASK: HOW DOES THIS LINK TO CONTEXT?

ASK: DO OTHER QUOTATIONS LINK TO THIS?

"Solitary as an oyster."

FLASHCARD

TEAR THIS PAGE OUT, FILL THIS SIDE IN AND BINGO! YOU HAVE A FABULOUS FLASHCARD.

THIS QUOTATION IS FROM STAVE _____.

THE WORDS BELONG TO _____

_____.

ONE LITERARY TECHNIQUE USED IS

_____.

ANOTHER LITERARY TECHNIQUE USED IS

_____.

THE WORD CLASS OF THE KEY WORD

" _____ " IS _____.

WRITE THE QUOTATION HERE — MAKE SURE IT IS <u>EXACTLY</u> THE SAME AS IT IS ON THE OTHER SIDE!

ASK: HOW DOES THIS MAKE YOU FEEL?

ASK: WOULD VICTORIANS HAVE FELT THE SAME?

ASK: HOW DOES THIS LINK TO CONTEXT?

ASK: DO OTHER QUOTATIONS LINK TO THIS?

"A frosty rime was on his head."

FLASHCARD

THIS QUOTATION IS FROM STAVE _____.

THE WORDS BELONG TO _____

_____.

ONE LITERARY TECHNIQUE USED IS

_____.

ANOTHER LITERARY TECHNIQUE USED IS

_____.

THE WORD CLASS OF THE KEY WORD

" _____ " IS _____.

WRITE THE QUOTATION HERE — MAKE SURE IT IS <u>EXACTLY</u> THE SAME AS IT IS ON THE OTHER SIDE!

ASK: HOW DOES THIS MAKE YOU FEEL?

ASK: WOULD VICTORIANS HAVE FELT THE SAME?

ASK: HOW DOES THIS LINK TO CONTEXT?

ASK: DO OTHER QUOTATIONS LINK TO THIS?

"The clerk put on his white comforter, and tried to warm himself at the candle."

FLASHCARD

THIS QUOTATION IS FROM STAVE _____ .

THE WORDS BELONG TO _____

_____ .

ONE LITERARY TECHNIQUE USED IS

_____ .

ANOTHER LITERARY TECHNIQUE USED IS

_____ .

THE WORD CLASS OF THE KEY WORD

" _____ " IS _____ .

WRITE THE QUOTATION HERE — MAKE SURE IT IS <u>EXACTLY</u> THE SAME AS IT IS ON THE OTHER SIDE!

ASK: HOW DOES THIS MAKE YOU FEEL?

ASK: WOULD VICTORIANS HAVE FELT THE SAME?

ASK: HOW DOES THIS LINK TO CONTEXT?

ASK: DO OTHER QUOTATIONS LINK TO THIS?

"A merry Christmas, uncle! God save you!"
"'Bah!' said Scrooge, 'Humbug!'"

FLASHCARD

TEAR THIS PAGE OUT, FILL THIS SIDE IN AND BINGO! YOU HAVE A FABULOUS FLASHCARD.

THIS QUOTATION IS FROM STAVE _____ .

THE WORDS BELONG TO _____

_____ .

ONE LITERARY TECHNIQUE USED IS

_____ .

ANOTHER LITERARY TECHNIQUE USED IS

_____ .

THE WORD CLASS OF THE KEY WORD

" _____ " IS _____ .

WRITE THE QUOTATION HERE — MAKE SURE IT IS EXACTLY THE SAME AS IT IS ON THE OTHER SIDE!

ASK: HOW DOES THIS MAKE YOU FEEL?

ASK: WOULD VICTORIANS HAVE FELT THE SAME?

ASK: HOW DOES THIS LINK TO CONTEXT?

ASK: DO OTHER QUOTATIONS LINK TO THIS?

"Are there no prisons?"

FLASHCARD

TEAR THIS PAGE OUT, FILL THIS SIDE IN AND BINGO! YOU HAVE A FABULOUS FLASHCARD.

THIS QUOTATION IS FROM STAVE _____ .

THE WORDS BELONG TO _____

_____ .

ONE LITERARY TECHNIQUE USED IS

_____ .

ANOTHER LITERARY TECHNIQUE USED IS

_____ .

THE WORD CLASS OF THE KEY WORD

" _____ " IS _____ .

WRITE THE QUOTATION HERE — MAKE SURE IT IS EXACTLY THE SAME AS IT IS ON THE OTHER SIDE!

ASK: HOW DOES THIS MAKE YOU FEEL?

ASK: WOULD VICTORIANS HAVE FELT THE SAME?

ASK: HOW DOES THIS LINK TO CONTEXT?

ASK: DO OTHER QUOTATIONS LINK TO THIS?

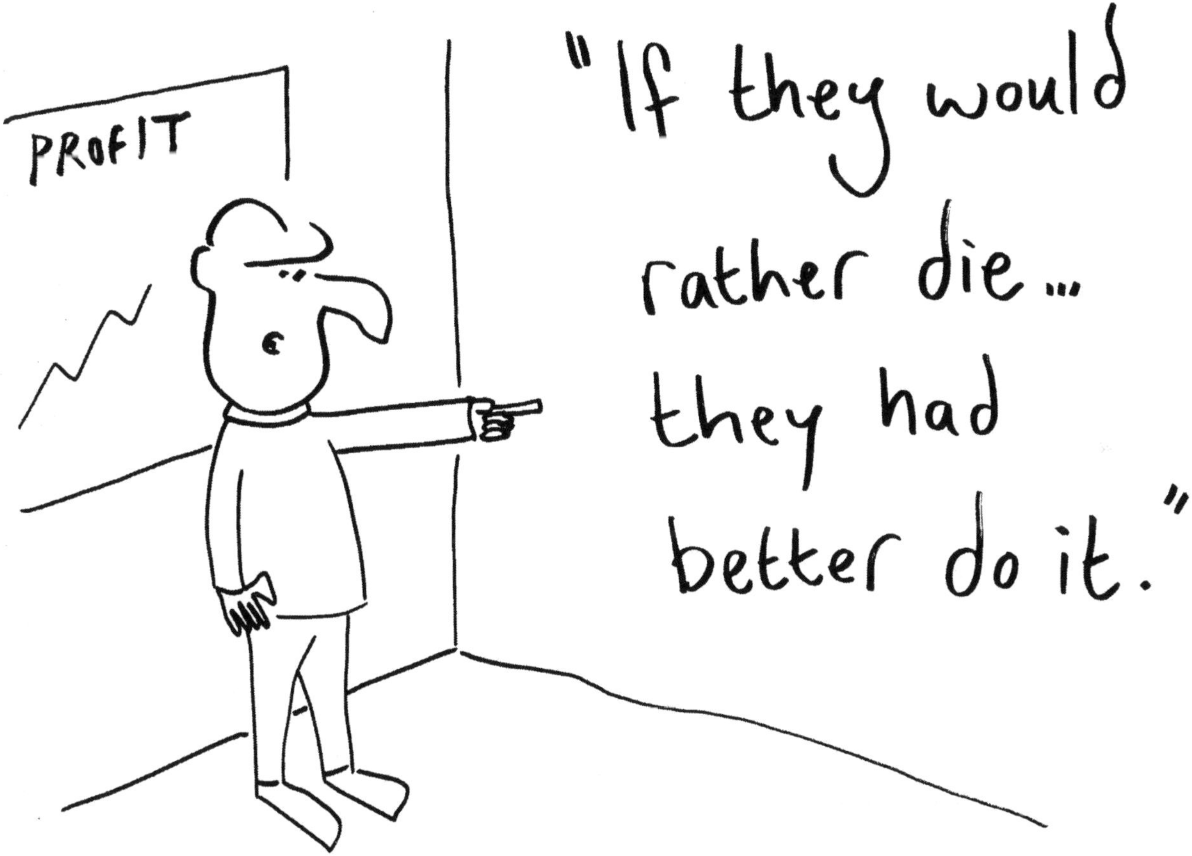
PROFIT
"If they would rather die... they had better do it."

FLASHCARD

TEAR THIS PAGE OUT, FILL THIS SIDE IN AND BINGO! YOU HAVE A FABULOUS FLASHCARD.

THIS QUOTATION IS FROM STAVE _____ .

THE WORDS BELONG TO _____

_____ .

ONE LITERARY TECHNIQUE USED IS

_____ .

ANOTHER LITERARY TECHNIQUE USED IS

_____ .

THE WORD CLASS OF THE KEY WORD

" _____ " IS _____ .

WRITE THE QUOTATION HERE — MAKE SURE IT IS EXACTLY THE SAME AS IT IS ON THE OTHER SIDE!

ASK: HOW DOES THIS MAKE YOU FEEL?

ASK: WOULD VICTORIANS HAVE FELT THE SAME?

ASK: HOW DOES THIS LINK TO CONTEXT?

ASK: DO OTHER QUOTATIONS LINK TO THIS?

Scrooge took his usual Melancholy dinner in his usual Melancholy tavern.

FLASHCARD

TEAR THIS PAGE OUT, FILL THIS SIDE IN AND BINGO! YOU HAVE A FABULOUS FLASHCARD.

THIS QUOTATION IS FROM STAVE _____ .

THE WORDS BELONG TO _____

_____ .

ONE LITERARY TECHNIQUE USED IS

_____ .

ANOTHER LITERARY TECHNIQUE USED IS

_____ .

THE WORD CLASS OF THE KEY WORD

" _____ " IS _____ .

WRITE THE QUOTATION HERE — MAKE SURE IT IS <u>EXACTLY</u> THE SAME AS IT IS ON THE OTHER SIDE!

ASK: HOW DOES THIS MAKE YOU FEEL?

ASK: WOULD VICTORIANS HAVE FELT THE SAME?

ASK: HOW DOES THIS LINK TO CONTEXT?

ASK: DO OTHER QUOTATIONS LINK TO THIS?

"A gloomy suite of rooms, in a lowering pile of building up a yard."

FLASHCARD

TEAR THIS PAGE OUT, FILL THIS SIDE IN AND BINGO! YOU HAVE A FABULOUS FLASHCARD.

THIS QUOTATION IS FROM STAVE _____.

THE WORDS BELONG TO _____

_____.

ONE LITERARY TECHNIQUE USED IS

_____.

ANOTHER LITERARY TECHNIQUE USED IS

_____.

THE WORD CLASS OF THE KEY WORD

" _____ " IS _____.

WRITE THE QUOTATION HERE — MAKE SURE IT IS <u>EXACTLY</u> THE SAME AS IT IS ON THE OTHER SIDE!

ASK: HOW DOES THIS MAKE YOU FEEL?

ASK: WOULD VICTORIANS HAVE FELT THE SAME?

ASK: HOW DOES THIS LINK TO CONTEXT?

ASK: DO OTHER QUOTATIONS LINK TO THIS?

"Not a knocker, but Marley's face."

FLASHCARD

TEAR THIS PAGE OUT, FILL THIS SIDE IN AND BINGO! YOU HAVE A FABULOUS FLASHCARD.

THIS QUOTATION IS FROM STAVE _____.

THE WORDS BELONG TO _____

_____.

ONE LITERARY TECHNIQUE USED IS

_____.

ANOTHER LITERARY TECHNIQUE USED IS

_____.

THE WORD CLASS OF THE KEY WORD

"_____" IS _____.

WRITE THE QUOTATION HERE — MAKE SURE IT IS EXACTLY THE SAME AS IT IS ON THE OTHER SIDE!

ASK: HOW DOES THIS MAKE YOU FEEL?
ASK: WOULD VICTORIANS HAVE FELT THE SAME?
ASK: HOW DOES THIS LINK TO CONTEXT?
ASK: DO OTHER QUOTATIONS LINK TO THIS?

"like a bad lobster in a dark cellar."

FLASHCARD

TEAR THIS PAGE OUT, FILL THIS SIDE IN AND BINGO! YOU HAVE A FABULOUS FLASHCARD.

THIS QUOTATION IS FROM STAVE _____ .

THE WORDS BELONG TO _____

_____ .

ONE LITERARY TECHNIQUE USED IS

_____ .

ANOTHER LITERARY TECHNIQUE USED IS

_____ .

THE WORD CLASS OF THE KEY WORD

" _____ " IS _____ .

WRITE THE QUOTATION HERE — MAKE SURE IT IS EXACTLY THE SAME AS IT IS ON THE OTHER SIDE!

ASK: HOW DOES THIS MAKE YOU FEEL?

ASK: WOULD VICTORIANS HAVE FELT THE SAME?

ASK: HOW DOES THIS LINK TO CONTEXT?

ASK: DO OTHER QUOTATIONS LINK TO THIS?

"Darkness is cheap,
and Scrooge liked it."

FLASHCARD

TEAR THIS PAGE OUT, FILL THIS SIDE IN AND BINGO! YOU HAVE A FABULOUS FLASHCARD.

THIS QUOTATION IS FROM STAVE _____.

THE WORDS BELONG TO _____

_____.

ONE LITERARY TECHNIQUE USED IS

_____.

ANOTHER LITERARY TECHNIQUE USED IS

_____.

THE WORD CLASS OF THE KEY WORD

" _____ " IS _____.

WRITE THE QUOTATION HERE — MAKE SURE IT IS EXACTLY THE SAME AS IT IS ON THE OTHER SIDE!

ASK: HOW DOES THIS MAKE YOU FEEL?
ASK: WOULD VICTORIANS HAVE FELT THE SAME?
ASK: HOW DOES THIS LINK TO CONTEXT?
ASK: DO OTHER QUOTATIONS LINK TO THIS?

FLASHCARD

TEAR THIS PAGE OUT, FILL THIS SIDE IN AND BINGO! YOU HAVE A FABULOUS FLASHCARD.

THIS QUOTATION IS FROM STAVE _____ .

THE WORDS BELONG TO _____

_____ .

ONE LITERARY TECHNIQUE USED IS

_____ .

ANOTHER LITERARY TECHNIQUE USED IS

_____ .

THE WORD CLASS OF THE KEY WORD

" _____ " IS _____ .

WRITE THE QUOTATION HERE — MAKE SURE IT IS EXACTLY THE SAME AS IT IS ON THE OTHER SIDE!

ASK: HOW DOES THIS MAKE YOU FEEL?

ASK: WOULD VICTORIANS HAVE FELT THE SAME?

ASK: HOW DOES THIS LINK TO CONTEXT?

ASK: DO OTHER QUOTATIONS LINK TO THIS?

"I have sat invisible beside you many and many a day."

FLASHCARD

THIS QUOTATION IS FROM STAVE _____ .

THE WORDS BELONG TO _____

_____ .

ONE LITERARY TECHNIQUE USED IS

_____ .

ANOTHER LITERARY TECHNIQUE USED IS

_____ .

THE WORD CLASS OF THE KEY WORD

" _____ " IS _____ .

WRITE THE QUOTATION HERE — MAKE SURE IT IS <u>EXACTLY</u> THE SAME AS IT IS ON THE OTHER SIDE!

ASK: HOW DOES THIS MAKE YOU FEEL?

ASK: WOULD VICTORIANS HAVE FELT THE SAME?

ASK: HOW DOES THIS LINK TO CONTEXT?

ASK: DO OTHER QUOTATIONS LINK TO THIS?

FLASHCARD

THIS QUOTATION IS FROM STAVE _____.

THE WORDS BELONG TO _____

_____.

ONE LITERARY TECHNIQUE USED IS

_____.

ANOTHER LITERARY TECHNIQUE USED IS

_____.

THE WORD CLASS OF THE KEY WORD

" _____ " IS _____.

WRITE THE QUOTATION HERE — MAKE SURE IT IS EXACTLY THE SAME AS IT IS ON THE OTHER SIDE!

ASK: HOW DOES THIS MAKE YOU FEEL?

ASK: WOULD VICTORIANS HAVE FELT THE SAME?

ASK: HOW DOES THIS LINK TO CONTEXT?

ASK: DO OTHER QUOTATIONS LINK TO THIS?

FLASHCARD

TEAR THIS PAGE OUT, FILL THIS SIDE IN AND BINGO! YOU HAVE A FABULOUS FLASHCARD.

THIS QUOTATION IS FROM STAVE _____.

THE WORDS BELONG TO _____

_____.

ONE LITERARY TECHNIQUE USED IS

_____.

ANOTHER LITERARY TECHNIQUE USED IS

_____.

THE WORD CLASS OF THE KEY WORD

" _____ " IS _____.

WRITE THE QUOTATION HERE — MAKE SURE IT IS <u>EXACTLY</u> THE SAME AS IT IS ON THE OTHER SIDE!

ASK: HOW DOES THIS MAKE YOU FEEL?

ASK: WOULD VICTORIANS HAVE FELT THE SAME?

ASK: HOW DOES THIS LINK TO CONTEXT?

ASK: DO OTHER QUOTATIONS LINK TO THIS?

"He had been quite familiar with one old ghost in a white waistcoat, with a monstrous iron safe attached to its ankle, who cried piteously at being unable to assist a wretched woman with an infant, whom it saw below upon a doorstep."

FLASHCARD

TEAR THIS PAGE OUT, FILL THIS SIDE IN AND BINGO! YOU HAVE A FABULOUS FLASHCARD.

THIS QUOTATION IS FROM STAVE _____.

THE WORDS BELONG TO _____

_____

ONE LITERARY TECHNIQUE USED IS

_____

ANOTHER LITERARY TECHNIQUE USED IS

_____

THE WORD CLASS OF THE KEY WORD

" _____ " IS _____.

WRITE THE QUOTATION HERE — MAKE SURE IT IS <u>EXACTLY</u> THE SAME AS IT IS ON THE OTHER SIDE!

ASK: HOW DOES THIS MAKE YOU FEEL?

ASK: WOULD VICTORIANS HAVE FELT THE SAME?

ASK: HOW DOES THIS LINK TO CONTEXT?

ASK: DO OTHER QUOTATIONS LINK TO THIS?

STAVE TWO:
THE FIRST OF THE
THREEEE
SPIRITS

FLASHCARD

STAVE TWO TIMELINE

Scrooge wakes in the dark.

"He could no more go to sleep than go to Heaven."

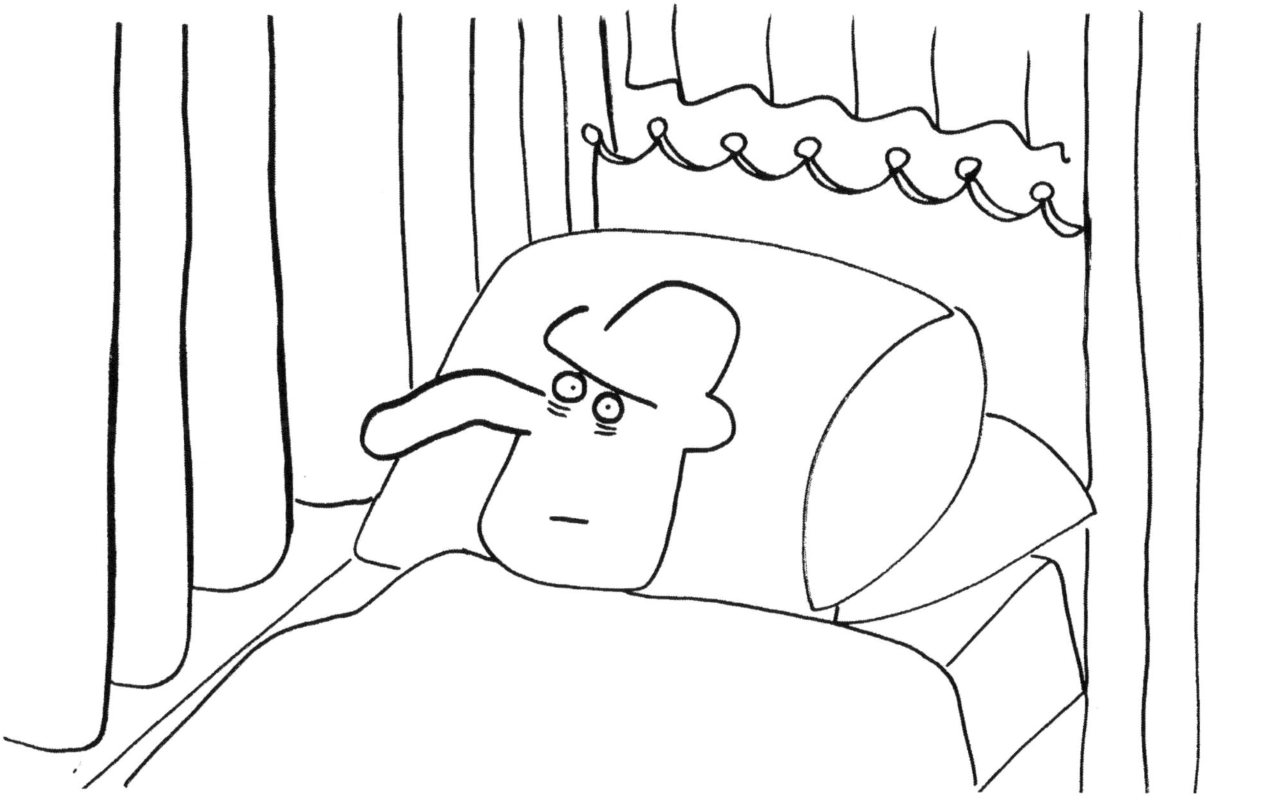

FLASHCARD

TEAR THIS PAGE OUT, FILL THIS SIDE IN AND BINGO! YOU HAVE A FABULOUS FLASHCARD.

THIS QUOTATION IS FROM STAVE _____.

THE WORDS BELONG TO _____

_____.

ONE LITERARY TECHNIQUE USED IS

_____.

ANOTHER LITERARY TECHNIQUE USED IS

_____.

THE WORD CLASS OF THE KEY WORD

" _____ " IS _____.

WRITE THE QUOTATION HERE — MAKE SURE IT IS <u>EXACTLY</u> THE SAME AS IT IS ON THE OTHER SIDE!

ASK: HOW DOES THIS MAKE YOU FEEL?

ASK: WOULD VICTORIANS HAVE FELT THE SAME?

ASK: HOW DOES THIS LINK TO CONTEXT?

ASK: DO OTHER QUOTATIONS LINK TO THIS?

"He spoke before the hour bell sounded, which it now did with a deep, dull, hollow, Melancholy ONE."

FLASHCARD

THIS QUOTATION IS FROM STAVE _____.

THE WORDS BELONG TO _____

_____.

ONE LITERARY TECHNIQUE USED IS

_____.

ANOTHER LITERARY TECHNIQUE USED IS

_____.

THE WORD CLASS OF THE KEY WORD

" _____ " IS _____.

WRITE THE QUOTATION HERE — MAKE SURE IT IS <u>EXACTLY</u> THE SAME AS IT IS ON THE OTHER SIDE!

ASK: HOW DOES THIS MAKE YOU FEEL?

ASK: WOULD VICTORIANS HAVE FELT THE SAME?

ASK: HOW DOES THIS LINK TO CONTEXT?

ASK: DO OTHER QUOTATIONS LINK TO THIS?

"The curtains of his bed were drawn aside, I tell you, by a hand."

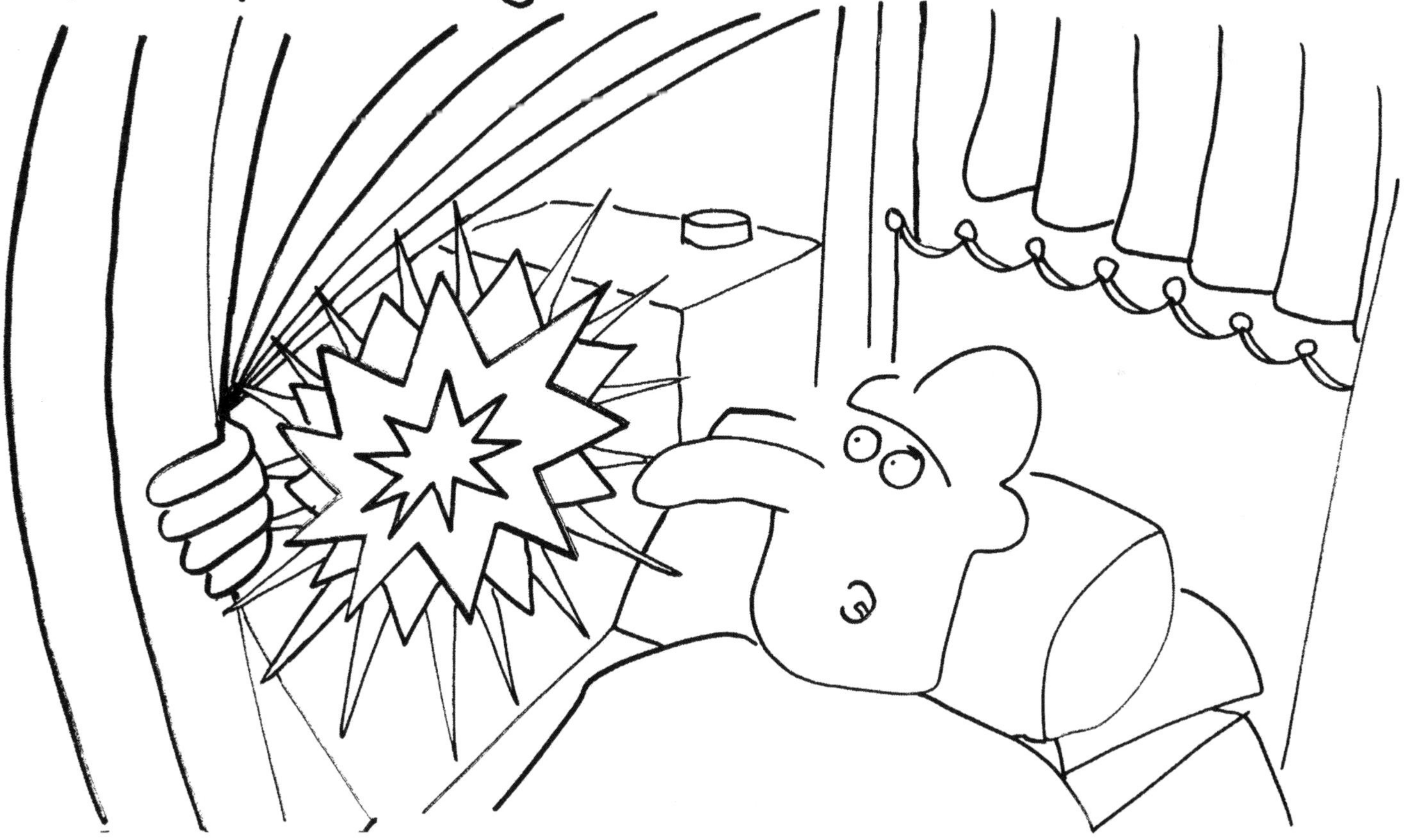

FLASHCARD

TEAR THIS PAGE OUT, FILL THIS SIDE IN AND BINGO! YOU HAVE A FABULOUS FLASHCARD.

THIS QUOTATION IS FROM STAVE _____.

THE WORDS BELONG TO _____

_____.

ONE LITERARY TECHNIQUE USED IS

_____.

ANOTHER LITERARY TECHNIQUE USED IS

_____.

THE WORD CLASS OF THE KEY WORD

" _____ " IS _____.

WRITE THE QUOTATION HERE — MAKE SURE IT IS <u>EXACTLY</u> THE SAME AS IT IS ON THE OTHER SIDE!

ASK: HOW DOES THIS MAKE YOU FEEL?

ASK: WOULD VICTORIANS HAVE FELT THE SAME?

ASK: HOW DOES THIS LINK TO CONTEXT?

ASK: DO OTHER QUOTATIONS LINK TO THIS?

"It was a strange figure — like a child; yet not so like a child as like an old man."

FLASHCARD

TEAR THIS PAGE OUT, FILL THIS SIDE IN AND BINGO! YOU HAVE A FABULOUS FLASHCARD.

THIS QUOTATION IS FROM STAVE _____.

THE WORDS BELONG TO _____

_____ _____.

ONE LITERARY TECHNIQUE USED IS

_____ _____.

ANOTHER LITERARY TECHNIQUE USED IS

_____ _____.

THE WORD CLASS OF THE KEY WORD

"_____" IS _____.

WRITE THE QUOTATION HERE — MAKE SURE IT IS <u>EXACTLY</u> THE SAME AS IT IS ON THE OTHER SIDE!

ASK: HOW DOES THIS MAKE YOU FEEL?

ASK: WOULD VICTORIANS HAVE FELT THE SAME?

ASK: HOW DOES THIS LINK TO CONTEXT?

ASK: DO OTHER QUOTATIONS LINK TO THIS?

"Would you so soon put out, with worldly hands, the

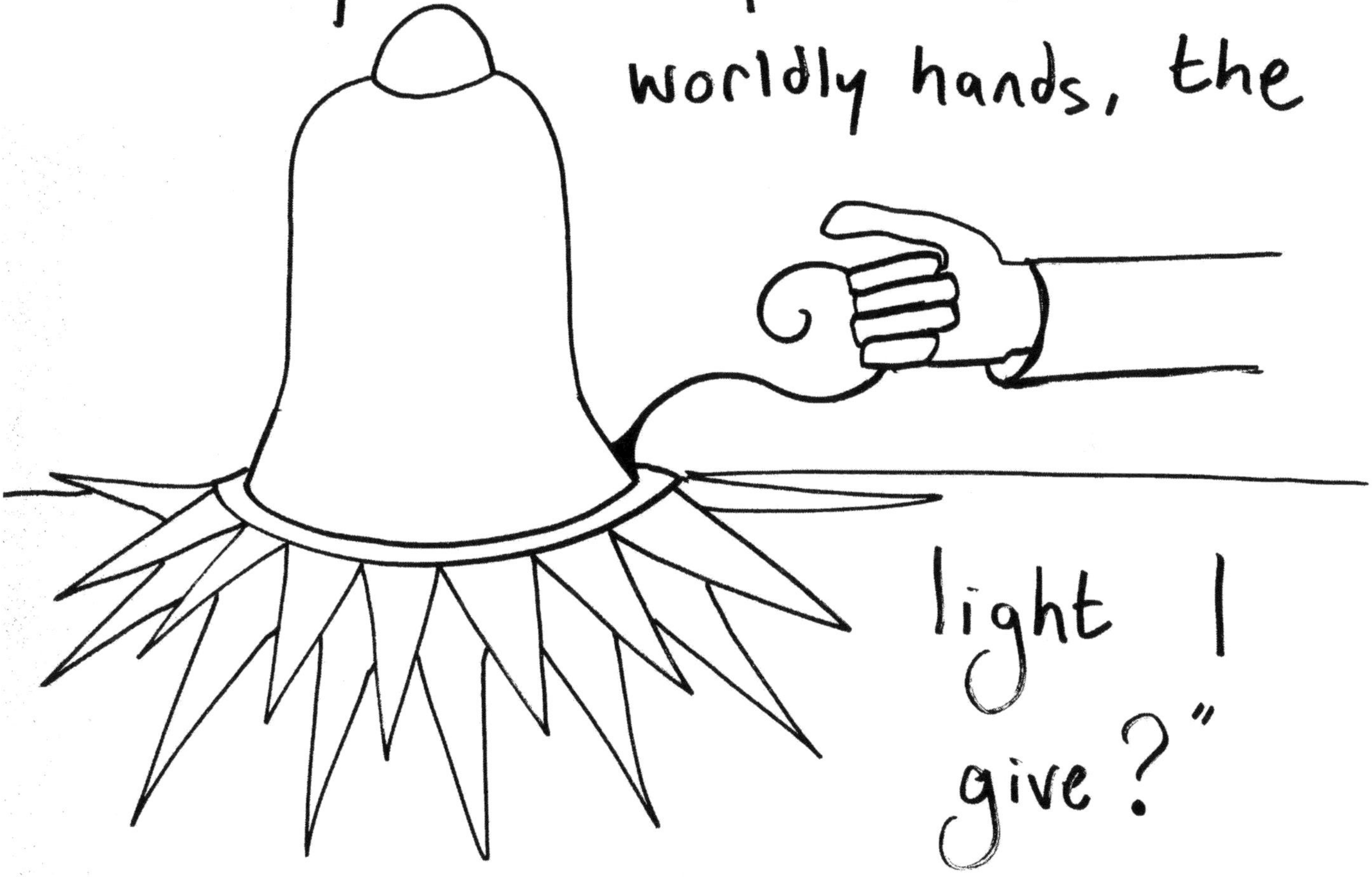

light I give?"

FLASHCARD

TEAR THIS PAGE OUT, FILL THIS SIDE IN AND BINGO! YOU HAVE A FABULOUS FLASHCARD.

THIS QUOTATION IS FROM STAVE _____.

THE WORDS BELONG TO _____

_____.

ONE LITERARY TECHNIQUE USED IS

_____.

ANOTHER LITERARY TECHNIQUE USED IS

_____.

THE WORD CLASS OF THE KEY WORD

" _____ " IS _____.

WRITE THE QUOTATION HERE — MAKE SURE IT IS <u>EXACTLY</u> THE SAME AS IT IS ON THE OTHER SIDE!

ASK: HOW DOES THIS MAKE YOU FEEL?

ASK: WOULD VICTORIANS HAVE FELT THE SAME?

ASK: HOW DOES THIS LINK TO CONTEXT?

ASK: DO OTHER QUOTATIONS LINK TO THIS?

"'I am a mortal,' Scrooge remonstrated, 'and liable to fall.'"

FLASHCARD

TEAR THIS PAGE OUT, FILL THIS SIDE IN AND BINGO! YOU HAVE A FABULOUS FLASHCARD.

THIS QUOTATION IS FROM STAVE _____ .

THE WORDS BELONG TO _____

_____ .

ONE LITERARY TECHNIQUE USED IS

_____ .

ANOTHER LITERARY TECHNIQUE USED IS

_____ .

THE WORD CLASS OF THE KEY WORD

" _____ " IS _____ .

WRITE THE QUOTATION HERE — MAKE SURE IT IS <u>EXACTLY</u> THE SAME AS IT IS ON THE OTHER SIDE!

ASK: HOW DOES THIS MAKE YOU FEEL?

ASK: WOULD VICTORIANS HAVE FELT THE SAME?

ASK: HOW DOES THIS LINK TO CONTEXT?

ASK: DO OTHER QUOTATIONS LINK TO THIS?

FLASHCARD

TEAR THIS PAGE OUT, FILL THIS SIDE IN AND BINGO! YOU HAVE A FABULOUS FLASHCARD.

THIS QUOTATION IS FROM STAVE _____ .

THE WORDS BELONG TO _____

_____ .

ONE LITERARY TECHNIQUE USED IS

_____ .

ANOTHER LITERARY TECHNIQUE USED IS

_____ .

THE WORD CLASS OF THE KEY WORD

" _____ " IS _____ .

WRITE THE QUOTATION HERE — MAKE SURE IT IS <u>EXACTLY</u> THE SAME AS IT IS ON THE OTHER SIDE!

ASK: HOW DOES THIS MAKE YOU FEEL?

ASK: WOULD VICTORIANS HAVE FELT THE SAME?

ASK: HOW DOES THIS LINK TO CONTEXT?

ASK: DO OTHER QUOTATIONS LINK TO THIS?

"A solitary child, neglected by his friends, is left there still."

FLASHCARD

TEAR THIS PAGE OUT, FILL THIS SIDE IN AND BINGO! YOU HAVE A FABULOUS FLASHCARD.

THIS QUOTATION IS FROM STAVE _____ .

THE WORDS BELONG TO _____

_____ .

ONE LITERARY TECHNIQUE USED IS

_____ .

ANOTHER LITERARY TECHNIQUE USED IS

_____ .

THE WORD CLASS OF THE KEY WORD

" _____ " IS _____ .

WRITE THE QUOTATION HERE — MAKE SURE IT IS <u>EXACTLY</u> THE SAME AS IT IS ON THE <u>OTHER</u> SIDE!

ASK: HOW DOES THIS MAKE YOU FEEL?

ASK: WOULD VICTORIANS HAVE FELT THE SAME?

ASK: HOW DOES THIS LINK TO CONTEXT?

ASK: DO OTHER QUOTATIONS LINK TO THIS?

"A long, bare, melancholy room, made barer still by lines of plain deal forms and desks."

FLASHCARD

TEAR THIS PAGE OUT, FILL THIS SIDE IN AND BINGO! YOU HAVE A FABULOUS FLASHCARD.

THIS QUOTATION IS FROM STAVE _____.

THE WORDS BELONG TO _____

_____.

ONE LITERARY TECHNIQUE USED IS

_____.

ANOTHER LITERARY TECHNIQUE USED IS

_____.

THE WORD CLASS OF THE KEY WORD

" _____ " IS _____.

WRITE THE QUOTATION HERE — MAKE SURE IT IS <u>EXACTLY</u> THE SAME AS IT IS ON THE OTHER SIDE!

ASK: HOW DOES THIS MAKE YOU FEEL?

ASK: WOULD VICTORIANS HAVE FELT THE SAME?

ASK: HOW DOES THIS LINK TO CONTEXT?

ASK: DO OTHER QUOTATIONS LINK TO THIS?

"I've come to bring you home, dear brother... home, home, home!"

FLASHCARD

TEAR THIS PAGE OUT, FILL THIS SIDE IN AND BINGO! YOU HAVE A FABULOUS FLASHCARD.

THIS QUOTATION IS FROM STAVE _____ .

THE WORDS BELONG TO _____

_____ .

ONE LITERARY TECHNIQUE USED IS

_____ .

ANOTHER LITERARY TECHNIQUE USED IS

_____ .

THE WORD CLASS OF THE KEY WORD

" _____ " IS _____ .

WRITE THE QUOTATION HERE — MAKE SURE IT IS <u>EXACTLY</u> THE SAME AS IT IS ON THE OTHER SIDE!

ASK: HOW DOES THIS MAKE YOU FEEL?

ASK: WOULD VICTORIANS HAVE FELT THE SAME?

ASK: HOW DOES THIS LINK TO CONTEXT?

ASK: DO OTHER QUOTATIONS LINK TO THIS?

"Father's so much kinder than he used to be, that home's like heaven!"

FLASHCARD

TEAR THIS PAGE OUT, FILL THIS SIDE IN AND BINGO! YOU HAVE A FABULOUS FLASHCARD.

THIS QUOTATION IS FROM STAVE _____ .

THE WORDS BELONG TO _____

_____ .

ONE LITERARY TECHNIQUE USED IS

_____ .

ANOTHER LITERARY TECHNIQUE USED IS

_____ .

THE WORD CLASS OF THE KEY WORD

" _____ " IS _____ .

WRITE THE QUOTATION HERE — MAKE SURE IT IS EXACTLY THE SAME AS IT IS ON THE OTHER SIDE!

ASK: HOW DOES THIS MAKE YOU FEEL?
ASK: WOULD VICTORIANS HAVE FELT THE SAME?
ASK: HOW DOES THIS LINK TO CONTEXT?
ASK: DO OTHER QUOTATIONS LINK TO THIS?

FLASHCARD

TEAR THIS PAGE OUT, FILL THIS SIDE IN AND BINGO! YOU HAVE A FABULOUS FLASHCARD.

THIS QUOTATION IS FROM STAVE _____ .

THE WORDS BELONG TO _____

_____ .

ONE LITERARY TECHNIQUE USED IS

_____ .

ANOTHER LITERARY TECHNIQUE USED IS

_____ .

THE WORD CLASS OF THE KEY WORD

" _____ " IS _____ .

WRITE THE QUOTATION HERE — MAKE SURE IT IS <u>EXACTLY</u> THE SAME AS IT IS ON THE <u>OTHER</u> SIDE!

ASK: HOW DOES THIS MAKE YOU FEEL?

ASK: WOULD VICTORIANS HAVE FELT THE SAME?

ASK: HOW DOES THIS LINK TO CONTEXT?

ASK: DO OTHER QUOTATIONS LINK TO THIS?

FLASHCARD

TEAR THIS PAGE OUT, FILL THIS SIDE IN AND BINGO! YOU HAVE A FABULOUS FLASHCARD.

THIS QUOTATION IS FROM STAVE _____.

THE WORDS BELONG TO _____

_____.

ONE LITERARY TECHNIQUE USED IS

_____.

ANOTHER LITERARY TECHNIQUE USED IS

_____.

THE WORD CLASS OF THE KEY WORD

" _____ " IS _____.

WRITE THE QUOTATION HERE — MAKE SURE IT IS <u>EXACTLY</u> THE SAME AS IT IS ON THE OTHER SIDE!

ASK: HOW DOES THIS MAKE YOU FEEL?

ASK: WOULD VICTORIANS HAVE FELT THE SAME?

ASK: HOW DOES THIS LINK TO CONTEXT?

ASK: DO OTHER QUOTATIONS LINK TO THIS?

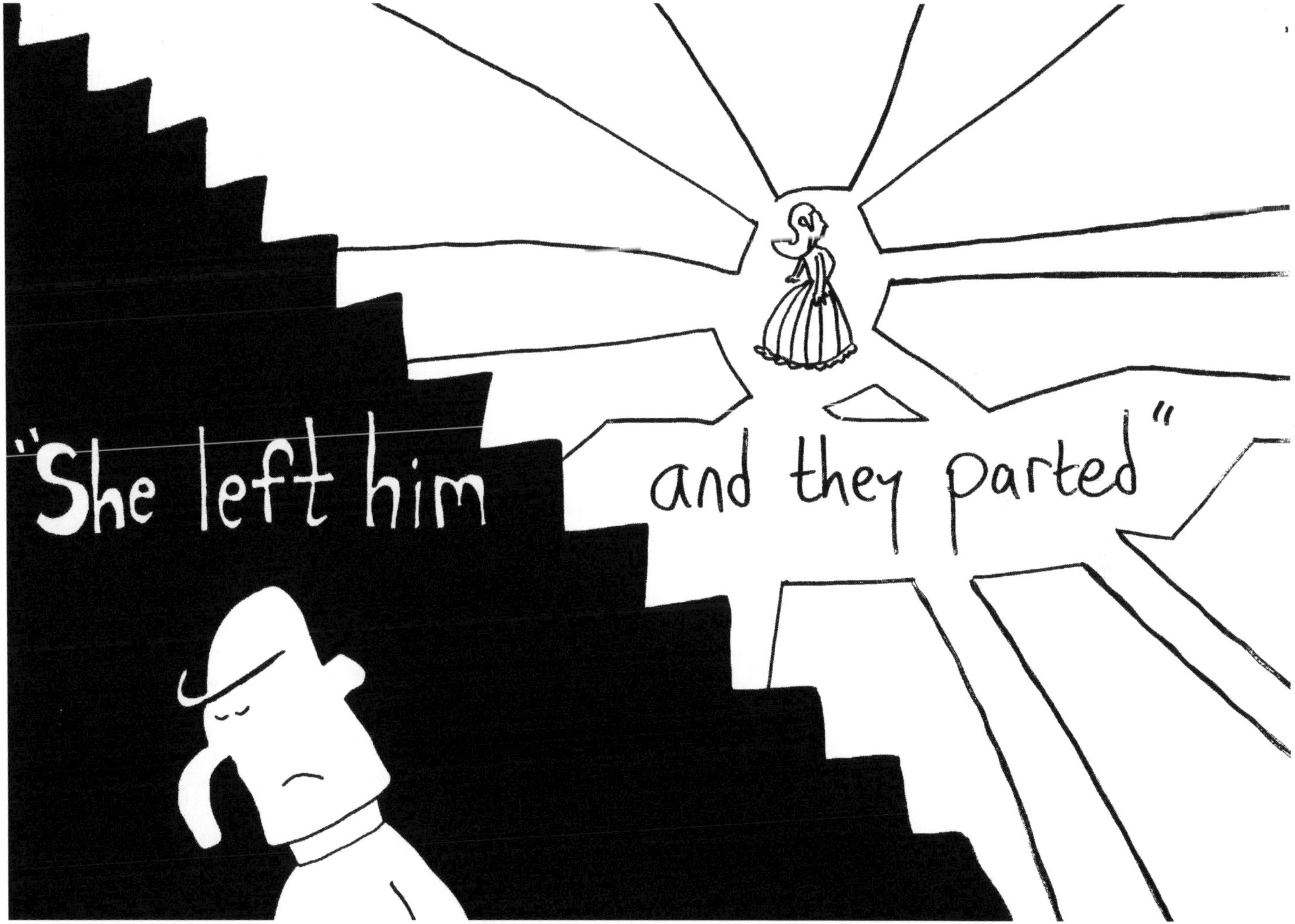
"She left him
and they parted"

FLASHCARD

THIS QUOTATION IS FROM STAVE _____.

THE WORDS BELONG TO _____

_____.

ONE LITERARY TECHNIQUE USED IS

_____.

ANOTHER LITERARY TECHNIQUE USED IS

_____.

THE WORD CLASS OF THE KEY WORD

" _____ " IS _____.

WRITE THE QUOTATION HERE — MAKE SURE IT IS <u>EXACTLY</u> THE SAME AS IT IS ON THE OTHER SIDE!

ASK: HOW DOES THIS MAKE YOU FEEL?

ASK: WOULD VICTORIANS HAVE FELT THE SAME?

ASK: HOW DOES THIS LINK TO CONTEXT?

ASK: DO OTHER QUOTATIONS LINK TO THIS?

"Quite alone in the world."

FLASHCARD

TEAR THIS PAGE OUT, FILL THIS SIDE IN AND BINGO! YOU HAVE A FABULOUS FLASHCARD.

THIS QUOTATION IS FROM STAVE _____.

THE WORDS BELONG TO _____

_____.

ONE LITERARY TECHNIQUE USED IS

_____.

ANOTHER LITERARY TECHNIQUE USED IS

_____.

THE WORD CLASS OF THE KEY WORD

" _____ " IS _____.

WRITE THE QUOTATION HERE — MAKE SURE IT IS <u>EXACTLY</u> THE SAME AS IT IS ON THE OTHER SIDE!

ASK: HOW DOES THIS MAKE YOU FEEL?

ASK: WOULD VICTORIANS HAVE FELT THE SAME?

ASK: HOW DOES THIS LINK TO CONTEXT?

ASK: DO OTHER QUOTATIONS LINK TO THIS?

STAVE THREE TIMELINE

A loud snore of Scrooge's wakes him up.

FLASHCARD

TEAR THIS PAGE OUT, FILL THIS SIDE IN AND BINGO! YOU HAVE A FABULOUS FLASHCARD.

THIS QUOTATION IS FROM STAVE _____.

THE WORDS BELONG TO _____

_____.

ONE LITERARY TECHNIQUE USED IS

_____.

ANOTHER LITERARY TECHNIQUE USED IS

_____.

THE WORD CLASS OF THE KEY WORD

" _____ " IS _____.

WRITE THE QUOTATION HERE — MAKE SURE IT IS <u>EXACTLY</u> THE SAME AS IT IS ON THE OTHER SIDE!

ASK: HOW DOES THIS MAKE YOU FEEL?
ASK: WOULD VICTORIANS HAVE FELT THE SAME?
ASK: HOW DOES THIS LINK TO CONTEXT?
ASK: DO OTHER QUOTATIONS LINK TO THIS?

"The moment Scrooge's hand was on the lock, a strange voice called him by his name."

FLASHCARD

TEAR THIS PAGE OUT, FILL THIS SIDE IN AND BINGO! YOU HAVE A FABULOUS FLASHCARD.

THIS QUOTATION IS FROM STAVE _____ .

THE WORDS BELONG TO _____

_____ .

ONE LITERARY TECHNIQUE USED IS

_____ .

ANOTHER LITERARY TECHNIQUE USED IS

_____ .

THE WORD CLASS OF THE KEY WORD

" _____ " IS _____ .

WRITE THE QUOTATION HERE — MAKE SURE IT IS EXACTLY THE SAME AS IT IS ON THE OTHER SIDE!

ASK: HOW DOES THIS MAKE YOU FEEL?

ASK: WOULD VICTORIANS HAVE FELT THE SAME?

ASK: HOW DOES THIS LINK TO CONTEXT?

ASK: DO OTHER QUOTATIONS LINK TO THIS?

FLASHCARD

THIS QUOTATION IS FROM STAVE _____ .

THE WORDS BELONG TO _____

_____ .

ONE LITERARY TECHNIQUE USED IS

_____ .

ANOTHER LITERARY TECHNIQUE USED IS

_____ .

THE WORD CLASS OF THE KEY WORD

" _____ " IS _____ .

WRITE THE QUOTATION HERE — MAKE SURE IT IS <u>EXACTLY</u> THE SAME AS IT IS ON THE OTHER SIDE!

ASK: HOW DOES THIS MAKE YOU FEEL?

ASK: WOULD VICTORIANS HAVE FELT THE SAME?

ASK: HOW DOES THIS LINK TO CONTEXT?

ASK: DO OTHER QUOTATIONS LINK TO THIS?

"Its dark brown curls were long and free; free as its genial face, its sparkling eye, its open hand, its cheery voice."

FLASHCARD

TEAR THIS PAGE OUT, FILL THIS SIDE IN AND BINGO! YOU HAVE A FABULOUS FLASHCARD.

THIS QUOTATION IS FROM STAVE _____.

THE WORDS BELONG TO _____

_____.

ONE LITERARY TECHNIQUE USED IS

_____.

ANOTHER LITERARY TECHNIQUE USED IS

_____.

THE WORD CLASS OF THE KEY WORD

" _____ " IS _____.

WRITE THE QUOTATION HERE — MAKE SURE IT IS <u>EXACTLY</u> THE SAME AS IT IS ON THE OTHER SIDE!

ASK: HOW DOES THIS MAKE YOU FEEL?

ASK: WOULD VICTORIANS HAVE FELT THE SAME?

ASK: HOW DOES THIS LINK TO CONTEXT?

ASK: DO OTHER QUOTATIONS LINK TO THIS?

"The Grocers'! oh, the Grocers'!"

FLASHCARD

TEAR THIS PAGE OUT, FILL THIS SIDE IN AND BINGO! YOU HAVE A FABULOUS FLASHCARD.

THIS QUOTATION IS FROM STAVE _____.

THE WORDS BELONG TO _____

_____.

ONE LITERARY TECHNIQUE USED IS

_____.

ANOTHER LITERARY TECHNIQUE USED IS

_____.

THE WORD CLASS OF THE KEY WORD

" _____ " IS _____.

WRITE THE QUOTATION HERE — MAKE SURE IT IS <u>EXACTLY</u> THE SAME AS IT IS ON THE OTHER SIDE!

ASK: HOW DOES THIS MAKE YOU FEEL?

ASK: WOULD VICTORIANS HAVE FELT THE SAME?

ASK: HOW DOES THIS LINK TO CONTEXT?

ASK: DO OTHER QUOTATIONS LINK TO THIS?

"The Ghost of Christmas Present
blessed his four-roomed house."
RC

FLASHCARD

THIS QUOTATION IS FROM STAVE _____ .

THE WORDS BELONG TO _____
_____ .

ONE LITERARY TECHNIQUE USED IS
_____ .

ANOTHER LITERARY TECHNIQUE USED IS
_____ .

THE WORD CLASS OF THE KEY WORD

" _____ " IS _____ .

WRITE THE QUOTATION HERE — MAKE SURE IT IS EXACTLY THE SAME AS IT IS ON THE OTHER SIDE!

ASK: HOW DOES THIS MAKE YOU FEEL?

ASK: WOULD VICTORIANS HAVE FELT THE SAME?

ASK: HOW DOES THIS LINK TO CONTEXT?

ASK: DO OTHER QUOTATIONS LINK TO THIS?

"Alas for Tiny Tim, he bore a little crutch, and had his limbs supported by an iron frame."

FLASHCARD

TEAR THIS PAGE OUT, FILL THIS SIDE IN AND BINGO! YOU HAVE A FABULOUS FLASHCARD.

THIS QUOTATION IS FROM STAVE _____.

THE WORDS BELONG TO _____

_____.

ONE LITERARY TECHNIQUE USED IS

_____.

ANOTHER LITERARY TECHNIQUE USED IS

_____.

THE WORD CLASS OF THE KEY WORD

" _____ " IS _____.

WRITE THE QUOTATION HERE — MAKE SURE IT IS <u>EXACTLY</u> THE SAME AS IT IS ON THE OTHER SIDE!

ASK: HOW DOES THIS MAKE YOU FEEL?

ASK: WOULD VICTORIANS HAVE FELT THE SAME?

ASK: HOW DOES THIS LINK TO CONTEXT?

ASK: DO OTHER QUOTATIONS LINK TO THIS?

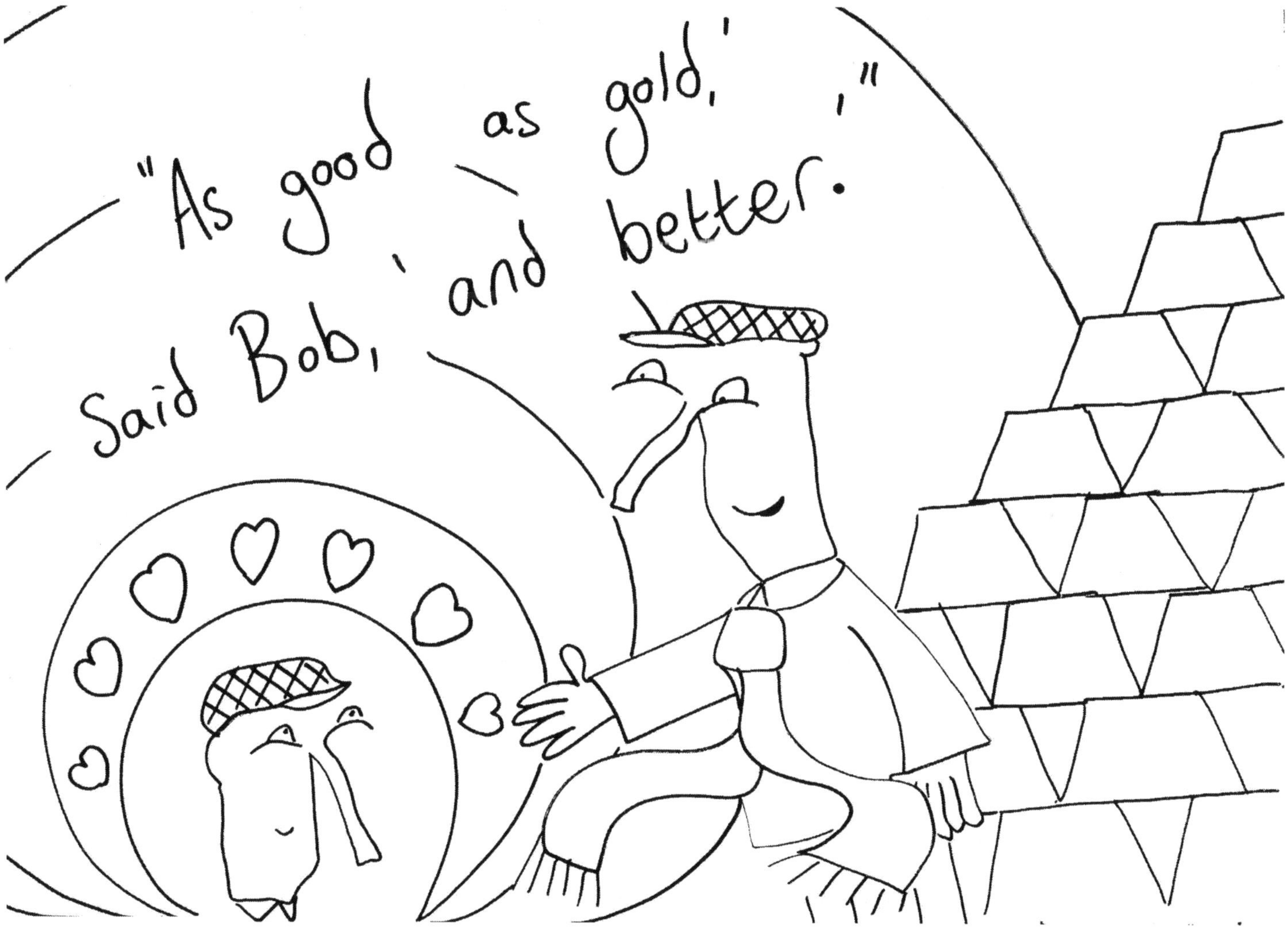
"As good as gold,' Said Bob, 'and better.'"

FLASHCARD

TEAR THIS PAGE OUT, FILL THIS SIDE IN AND BINGO! YOU HAVE A FABULOUS FLASHCARD.

THIS QUOTATION IS FROM STAVE _____ .

THE WORDS BELONG TO _____

_____ .

ONE LITERARY TECHNIQUE USED IS

_____ .

ANOTHER LITERARY TECHNIQUE USED IS

_____ .

THE WORD CLASS OF THE KEY WORD

" _____ " IS _____ .

WRITE THE QUOTATION HERE — MAKE SURE IT IS <u>EXACTLY</u> THE SAME AS IT IS ON THE OTHER SIDE!

ASK: HOW DOES THIS MAKE YOU FEEL?

ASK: WOULD VICTORIANS HAVE FELT THE SAME?

ASK: HOW DOES THIS LINK TO CONTEXT?

ASK: DO OTHER QUOTATIONS LINK TO THIS?

FLASHCARD

TEAR THIS PAGE OUT, FILL THIS SIDE IN AND BINGO! YOU HAVE A FABULOUS FLASHCARD.

THIS QUOTATION IS FROM STAVE _____.

THE WORDS BELONG TO _____

_____.

ONE LITERARY TECHNIQUE USED IS

_____.

ANOTHER LITERARY TECHNIQUE USED IS

_____.

THE WORD CLASS OF THE KEY WORD

" _____ " IS _____.

WRITE THE QUOTATION HERE — MAKE SURE IT IS EXACTLY THE SAME AS IT IS ON THE OTHER SIDE!

ASK: HOW DOES THIS MAKE YOU FEEL?
ASK: WOULD VICTORIANS HAVE FELT THE SAME?
ASK: HOW DOES THIS LINK TO CONTEXT?
ASK: DO OTHER QUOTATIONS LINK TO THIS?

"The family display of glass. Two tumblers and a custard cup without a handle."

FLASHCARD

TEAR THIS PAGE OUT, FILL THIS SIDE IN AND BINGO! YOU HAVE A FABULOUS FLASHCARD.

THIS QUOTATION IS FROM STAVE _____.

THE WORDS BELONG TO _____

_____.

ONE LITERARY TECHNIQUE USED IS

_____.

ANOTHER LITERARY TECHNIQUE USED IS

_____.

THE WORD CLASS OF THE KEY WORD

" _____ " IS _____.

WRITE THE QUOTATION HERE — MAKE SURE IT IS <u>EXACTLY</u> THE SAME AS IT IS ON THE <u>OTHER</u> SIDE!

ASK: HOW DOES THIS MAKE YOU FEEL?

ASK: WOULD VICTORIANS HAVE FELT THE SAME?

ASK: HOW DOES THIS LINK TO CONTEXT?

ASK: DO OTHER QUOTATIONS LINK TO THIS?

"Scrooge was the Ogre of the family."

FLASHCARD

TEAR THIS PAGE OUT, FILL THIS SIDE IN AND BINGO! YOU HAVE A FABULOUS FLASHCARD.

THIS QUOTATION IS FROM STAVE _____.

THE WORDS BELONG TO _____

_____.

ONE LITERARY TECHNIQUE USED IS

_____.

ANOTHER LITERARY TECHNIQUE USED IS

_____.

THE WORD CLASS OF THE KEY WORD

" _____ " IS _____.

WRITE THE QUOTATION HERE — MAKE SURE IT IS EXACTLY THE SAME AS IT IS ON THE OTHER SIDE!

ASK: HOW DOES THIS MAKE YOU FEEL?
ASK: WOULD VICTORIANS HAVE FELT THE SAME?
ASK: HOW DOES THIS LINK TO CONTEXT?
ASK: DO OTHER QUOTATIONS LINK TO THIS?

"Tell me if Tiny Tim
will live."

FLASHCARD

TEAR THIS PAGE OUT, FILL THIS SIDE IN AND BINGO! YOU HAVE A FABULOUS FLASHCARD.

THIS QUOTATION IS FROM STAVE _____.

THE WORDS BELONG TO _____

_____.

ONE LITERARY TECHNIQUE USED IS

_____.

ANOTHER LITERARY TECHNIQUE USED IS

_____.

THE WORD CLASS OF THE KEY WORD

" _____ " IS _____.

WRITE THE QUOTATION HERE — MAKE SURE IT IS EXACTLY THE SAME AS IT IS ON THE OTHER SIDE!

ASK: HOW DOES THIS MAKE YOU FEEL?
ASK: WOULD VICTORIANS HAVE FELT THE SAME?
ASK: HOW DOES THIS LINK TO CONTEXT?
ASK: DO OTHER QUOTATIONS LINK TO THIS?

"Ha, ha! Ha, ha, ha, ha!"

FLASHCARD

THIS QUOTATION IS FROM STAVE _____.

THE WORDS BELONG TO _____

_____.

ONE LITERARY TECHNIQUE USED IS

_____.

ANOTHER LITERARY TECHNIQUE USED IS

_____

THE WORD CLASS OF THE KEY WORD

" _____ " IS _____.

WRITE THE QUOTATION HERE — MAKE SURE IT IS EXACTLY THE SAME AS IT IS ON THE OTHER SIDE!

ASK: HOW DOES THIS MAKE YOU FEEL?
ASK: WOULD VICTORIANS HAVE FELT THE SAME?
ASK: HOW DOES THIS LINK TO CONTEXT?
ASK: DO OTHER QUOTATIONS LINK TO THIS?

an animal
a disagreeable animal
a live animal
cat
an ass
bear
tiger
bull
a savage
al
growled and grunted
wasn't led
not a horse
an ani
led in
neve
dog
a
a pig
a cow

FLASHCARD

TEAR THIS PAGE OUT, FILL THIS SIDE IN AND BINGO! YOU HAVE A FABULOUS FLASHCARD.

THIS QUOTATION IS FROM STAVE _____.

THE WORDS BELONG TO _____

_____.

ONE LITERARY TECHNIQUE USED IS

_____.

ANOTHER LITERARY TECHNIQUE USED IS

_____

THE WORD CLASS OF THE KEY WORD

" _____ " IS _____.

WRITE THE QUOTATION HERE — MAKE SURE IT IS EXACTLY THE SAME AS IT IS ON THE OTHER SIDE!

ASK: HOW DOES THIS MAKE YOU FEEL?
ASK: WOULD VICTORIANS HAVE FELT THE SAME?
ASK: HOW DOES THIS LINK TO CONTEXT?
ASK: DO OTHER QUOTATIONS LINK TO THIS?

" Is it a foot
or a claw? "

FLASHCARD

TEAR THIS PAGE OUT, FILL THIS SIDE IN AND BINGO! YOU HAVE A FABULOUS FLASHCARD.

THIS QUOTATION IS FROM STAVE _____.

THE WORDS BELONG TO _____

_____.

ONE LITERARY TECHNIQUE USED IS

_____.

ANOTHER LITERARY TECHNIQUE USED IS

_____

THE WORD CLASS OF THE KEY WORD

" _____ " IS _____.

WRITE THE QUOTATION HERE — MAKE SURE IT IS EXACTLY THE SAME AS IT IS ON THE OTHER SIDE!

ASK: HOW DOES THIS MAKE YOU FEEL?
ASK: WOULD VICTORIANS HAVE FELT THE SAME?
ASK: HOW DOES THIS LINK TO CONTEXT?
ASK: DO OTHER QUOTATIONS LINK TO THIS?

FLASHCARD

TEAR THIS PAGE OUT, FILL THIS SIDE IN AND BINGO! YOU HAVE A FABULOUS FLASHCARD.

THIS QUOTATION IS FROM STAVE _____.

THE WORDS BELONG TO _____

_____.

ONE LITERARY TECHNIQUE USED IS

_____.

ANOTHER LITERARY TECHNIQUE USED IS

_____.

THE WORD CLASS OF THE KEY WORD

" _____ " IS _____.

WRITE THE QUOTATION HERE — MAKE SURE IT IS <u>EXACTLY</u> THE SAME AS IT IS ON THE <u>OTHER</u> SIDE!

ASK: HOW DOES THIS MAKE YOU FEEL?
ASK: WOULD VICTORIANS HAVE FELT THE SAME?
ASK: HOW DOES THIS LINK TO CONTEXT?
ASK: DO OTHER QUOTATIONS LINK TO THIS?

STAVE FOUR: THE LAST OF THE SPIRITS

FLASHCARD

STAVE FOUR TIMELINE

The Phantom approaches.

"A solemn Phantom, draped and hooded."

"The Phantom slowly, gravely, silently approached."

FLASHCARD

TEAR THIS PAGE OUT, FILL THIS SIDE IN AND BINGO! YOU HAVE A FABULOUS FLASHCARD.

THIS QUOTATION IS FROM STAVE _____.

THE WORDS BELONG TO _____

_____.

ONE LITERARY TECHNIQUE USED IS

_____.

ANOTHER LITERARY TECHNIQUE USED IS

_____.

THE WORD CLASS OF THE KEY WORD

" _____ " IS _____.

WRITE THE QUOTATION HERE — MAKE SURE IT IS EXACTLY THE SAME AS IT IS ON THE OTHER SIDE!

ASK: HOW DOES THIS MAKE YOU FEEL?
ASK: WOULD VICTORIANS HAVE FELT THE SAME?
ASK: HOW DOES THIS LINK TO CONTEXT?
ASK: DO OTHER QUOTATIONS LINK TO THIS?

FLASHCARD

TEAR THIS PAGE OUT, FILL THIS SIDE IN AND BINGO! YOU HAVE A FABULOUS FLASHCARD.

THIS QUOTATION IS FROM STAVE _____.

THE WORDS BELONG TO _____

_____.

ONE LITERARY TECHNIQUE USED IS

_____.

ANOTHER LITERARY TECHNIQUE USED IS

_____.

THE WORD CLASS OF THE KEY WORD

" _____ " IS _____.

WRITE THE QUOTATION HERE — MAKE SURE IT IS <u>EXACTLY</u> THE SAME AS IT IS ON THE <u>OTHER</u> SIDE!

ASK: HOW DOES THIS MAKE YOU FEEL?

ASK: WOULD VICTORIANS HAVE FELT THE SAME?

ASK: HOW DOES THIS LINK TO CONTEXT?

ASK: DO OTHER QUOTATIONS LINK TO THIS?

"The people half naked, drunken,
Slipshod, ugly."

FLASHCARD

TEAR THIS PAGE OUT, FILL THIS SIDE IN AND BINGO! YOU HAVE A FABULOUS FLASHCARD.

THIS QUOTATION IS FROM STAVE _____.

THE WORDS BELONG TO _____

_____.

ONE LITERARY TECHNIQUE USED IS

_____.

ANOTHER LITERARY TECHNIQUE USED IS

_____.

THE WORD CLASS OF THE KEY WORD

" _____ " IS _____.

WRITE THE QUOTATION HERE — MAKE SURE IT IS <u>EXACTLY</u> THE SAME AS IT IS ON THE OTHER SIDE!

ASK: HOW DOES THIS MAKE YOU FEEL?

ASK: WOULD VICTORIANS HAVE FELT THE SAME?

ASK: HOW DOES THIS LINK TO CONTEXT?

ASK: DO OTHER QUOTATIONS LINK TO THIS?

"The whole quarter reeked with crime, with filth, and misery."

FLASHCARD

TEAR THIS PAGE OUT, FILL THIS SIDE IN AND BINGO! YOU HAVE A FABULOUS FLASHCARD.

THIS QUOTATION IS FROM STAVE _____.

THE WORDS BELONG TO _____

_____.

ONE LITERARY TECHNIQUE USED IS

_____.

ANOTHER LITERARY TECHNIQUE USED IS

_____.

THE WORD CLASS OF THE KEY WORD

" _____ " IS _____.

WRITE THE QUOTATION HERE — MAKE SURE IT IS EXACTLY THE SAME AS IT IS ON THE OTHER SIDE!

ASK: HOW DOES THIS MAKE YOU FEEL?

ASK: WOULD VICTORIANS HAVE FELT THE SAME?

ASK: HOW DOES THIS LINK TO CONTEXT?

ASK: DO OTHER QUOTATIONS LINK TO THIS?

"Far in this den of infamous resort, there was a lowbrowed, beetling shop."

FLASHCARD

THIS QUOTATION IS FROM STAVE _____.

THE WORDS BELONG TO _____
_____.

ONE LITERARY TECHNIQUE USED IS
_____.

ANOTHER LITERARY TECHNIQUE USED IS

_____.

THE WORD CLASS OF THE KEY WORD

" _____ " IS _____.

WRITE THE QUOTATION HERE — MAKE SURE IT IS EXACTLY THE SAME AS IT IS ON THE OTHER SIDE!

ASK: HOW DOES THIS MAKE YOU FEEL?
ASK: WOULD VICTORIANS HAVE FELT THE SAME?
ASK: HOW DOES THIS LINK TO CONTEXT?
ASK: DO OTHER QUOTATIONS LINK TO THIS?

"Secrets that few would like to scrutinise were bred and hidden in Mountains of unseemly rags, Masses of corrupted fat, and Sepulchres of bones."

FLASHCARD

TEAR THIS PAGE OUT, FILL THIS SIDE IN AND BINGO! YOU HAVE A FABULOUS FLASHCARD.

THIS QUOTATION IS FROM STAVE _____.

THE WORDS BELONG TO _____

_____.

ONE LITERARY TECHNIQUE USED IS

_____.

ANOTHER LITERARY TECHNIQUE USED IS

_____.

THE WORD CLASS OF THE KEY WORD

" _____ " IS _____.

WRITE THE QUOTATION HERE — MAKE SURE IT IS EXACTLY THE SAME AS IT IS ON THE OTHER SIDE!

ASK: HOW DOES THIS MAKE YOU FEEL?
ASK: WOULD VICTORIANS HAVE FELT THE SAME?
ASK: HOW DOES THIS LINK TO CONTEXT?
ASK: DO OTHER QUOTATIONS LINK TO THIS?

"They'd have wasted it,
if it hadn't been for me."

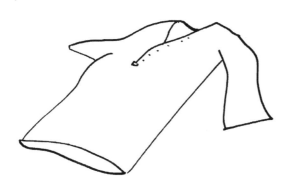

"Putting it on him to be buried
in... I took it off again."

FLASHCARD

TEAR THIS PAGE OUT, FILL THIS SIDE IN AND BINGO! YOU HAVE A FABULOUS FLASHCARD.

THIS QUOTATION IS FROM STAVE _____.

THE WORDS BELONG TO _____

_____.

ONE LITERARY TECHNIQUE USED IS

_____.

ANOTHER LITERARY TECHNIQUE USED IS

_____.

THE WORD CLASS OF THE KEY WORD

" _____ " IS _____.

WRITE THE QUOTATION HERE — MAKE SURE IT IS EXACTLY THE SAME AS IT IS ON THE OTHER SIDE!

ASK: HOW DOES THIS MAKE YOU FEEL?

ASK: WOULD VICTORIANS HAVE FELT THE SAME?

ASK: HOW DOES THIS LINK TO CONTEXT?

ASK: DO OTHER QUOTATIONS LINK TO THIS?

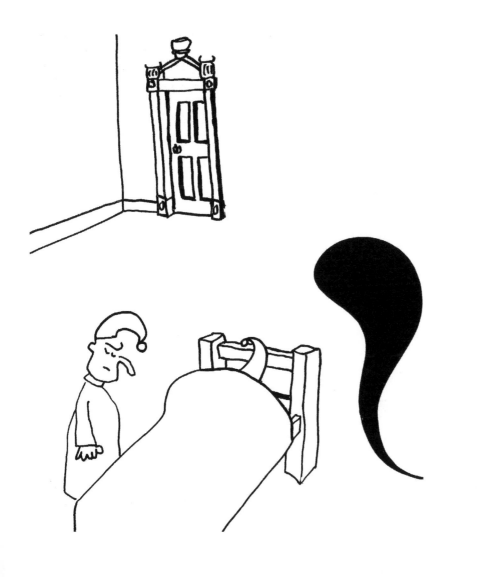

FLASHCARD

TEAR THIS PAGE OUT, FILL THIS SIDE IN AND BINGO! YOU HAVE A FABULOUS FLASHCARD.

THIS QUOTATION IS FROM STAVE _____.

THE WORDS BELONG TO _____

_____.

ONE LITERARY TECHNIQUE USED IS

_____.

ANOTHER LITERARY TECHNIQUE USED IS

_____.

THE WORD CLASS OF THE KEY WORD

" _____ " IS _____.

WRITE THE QUOTATION HERE — MAKE SURE IT IS <u>EXACTLY</u> THE SAME AS IT IS ON THE OTHER SIDE!

ASK: HOW DOES THIS MAKE YOU FEEL?

ASK: WOULD VICTORIANS HAVE FELT THE SAME?

ASK: HOW DOES THIS LINK TO CONTEXT?

ASK: DO OTHER QUOTATIONS LINK TO THIS?

"'My little, little child!' cried Bob. 'My little child!'"

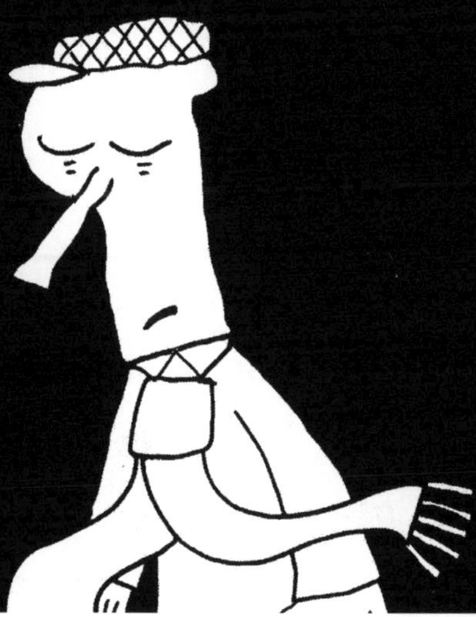

FLASHCARD

TEAR THIS PAGE OUT, FILL THIS SIDE IN AND BINGO! YOU HAVE A FABULOUS FLASHCARD.

THIS QUOTATION IS FROM STAVE _____.

THE WORDS BELONG TO _____

_____.

ONE LITERARY TECHNIQUE USED IS

_____.

ANOTHER LITERARY TECHNIQUE USED IS

_____.

THE WORD CLASS OF THE KEY WORD

" _____ " IS _____.

WRITE THE QUOTATION HERE — MAKE SURE IT IS <u>EXACTLY</u> THE SAME AS IT IS ON THE OTHER SIDE!

ASK: HOW DOES THIS MAKE YOU FEEL?
ASK: WOULD VICTORIANS HAVE FELT THE SAME?
ASK: HOW DOES THIS LINK TO CONTEXT?
ASK: DO OTHER QUOTATIONS LINK TO THIS?

"Spirit of Tiny Tim, thy childish essence was from God!"

FLASHCARD

TEAR THIS PAGE OUT, FILL THIS SIDE IN AND BINGO! YOU HAVE A FABULOUS FLASHCARD.

THIS QUOTATION IS FROM STAVE _____.

THE WORDS BELONG TO _____

_____.

ONE LITERARY TECHNIQUE USED IS

_____.

ANOTHER LITERARY TECHNIQUE USED IS

_____.

THE WORD CLASS OF THE KEY WORD

" _____ " IS _____.

WRITE THE QUOTATION HERE — MAKE SURE IT IS EXACTLY THE SAME AS IT IS ON THE OTHER SIDE!

ASK: HOW DOES THIS MAKE YOU FEEL?

ASK: WOULD VICTORIANS HAVE FELT THE SAME?

ASK: HOW DOES THIS LINK TO CONTEXT?

ASK: DO OTHER QUOTATIONS LINK TO THIS?

FLASHCARD

TEAR THIS PAGE OUT, FILL THIS SIDE IN AND BINGO! YOU HAVE A FABULOUS FLASHCARD.

THIS QUOTATION IS FROM STAVE _____ .

THE WORDS BELONG TO _____

_____ .

ONE LITERARY TECHNIQUE USED IS

_____ .

ANOTHER LITERARY TECHNIQUE USED IS

_____ .

THE WORD CLASS OF THE KEY WORD

" _____ " IS _____ .

WRITE THE QUOTATION HERE — MAKE SURE IT IS EXACTLY THE SAME AS IT IS ON THE OTHER SIDE!

ASK: HOW DOES THIS MAKE YOU FEEL?

ASK: WOULD VICTORIANS HAVE FELT THE SAME?

ASK: HOW DOES THIS LINK TO CONTEXT?

ASK: DO OTHER QUOTATIONS LINK TO THIS?

"Are these the shadows of the things that Will be, or are they shadows of things that May be only?"

FLASHCARD

TEAR THIS PAGE OUT, FILL THIS SIDE IN AND BINGO! YOU HAVE A FABULOUS FLASHCARD.

THIS QUOTATION IS FROM STAVE _____.

THE WORDS BELONG TO _____

_____.

ONE LITERARY TECHNIQUE USED IS

_____

ANOTHER LITERARY TECHNIQUE USED IS

_____

THE WORD CLASS OF THE KEY WORD

" _____ " IS _____.

WRITE THE QUOTATION HERE — MAKE SURE IT IS <u>EXACTLY</u> THE SAME AS IT IS ON THE OTHER SIDE!

ASK: HOW DOES THIS MAKE YOU FEEL?
ASK: WOULD VICTORIANS HAVE FELT THE SAME?
ASK: HOW DOES THIS LINK TO CONTEXT?
ASK: DO OTHER QUOTATIONS LINK TO THIS?

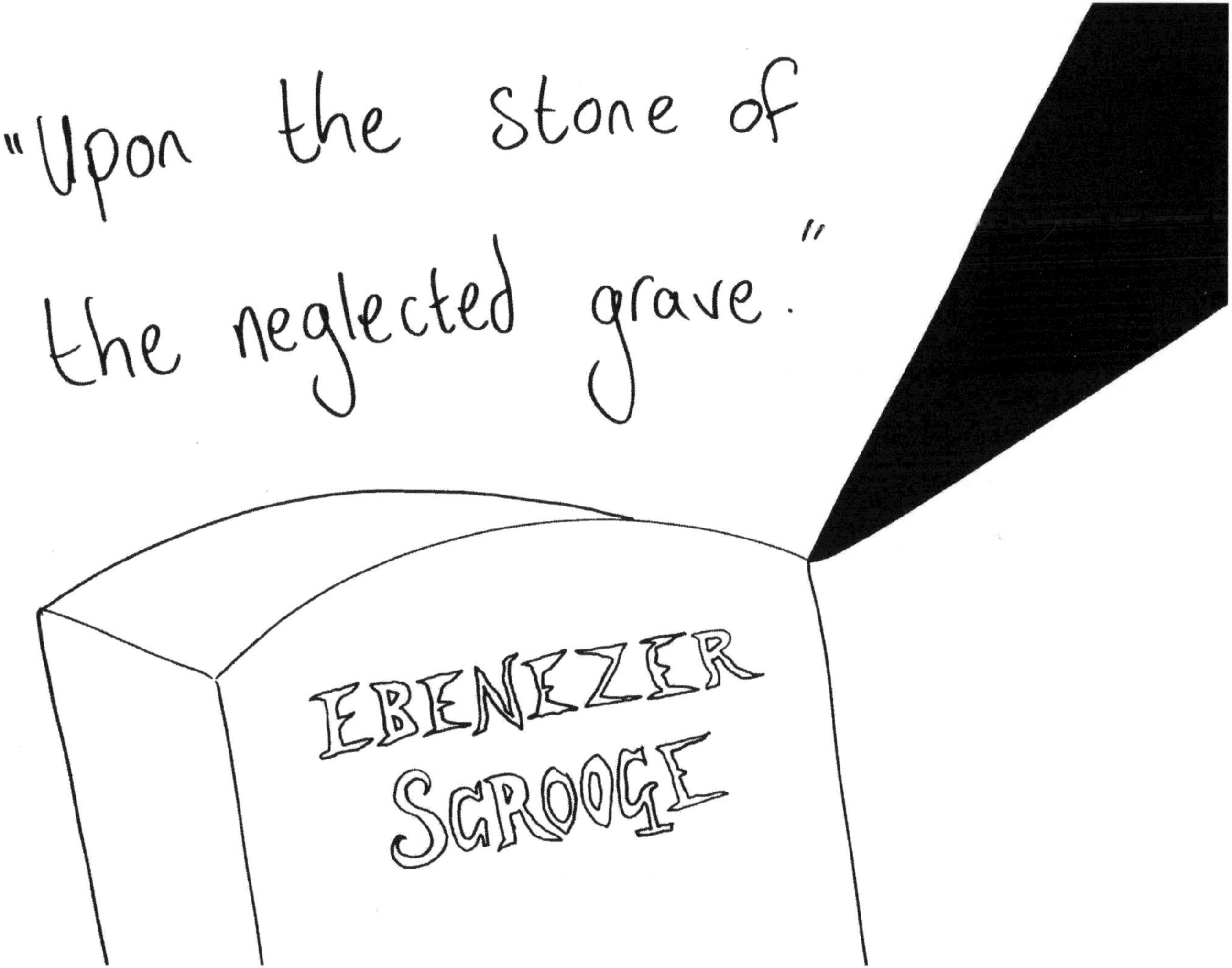
"Upon the stone of the neglected grave."
EBENEZER SCROOGE

FLASHCARD

TEAR THIS PAGE OUT, FILL THIS SIDE IN AND BINGO! YOU HAVE A FABULOUS FLASHCARD.

THIS QUOTATION IS FROM STAVE _____ .

THE WORDS BELONG TO _____

_____ .

ONE LITERARY TECHNIQUE USED IS

_____ .

ANOTHER LITERARY TECHNIQUE USED IS

_____ .

THE WORD CLASS OF THE KEY WORD

" _____ " IS _____ .

WRITE THE QUOTATION HERE — MAKE SURE IT IS <u>EXACTLY</u> THE SAME AS IT IS ON THE OTHER SIDE!

ASK: HOW DOES THIS MAKE YOU FEEL?

ASK: WOULD VICTORIANS HAVE FELT THE SAME?

ASK: HOW DOES THIS LINK TO CONTEXT?

ASK: DO OTHER QUOTATIONS LINK TO THIS?

"I will live in the Past, the Present, and the Future. The Spirits of all Three shall strive within Me."

FLASHCARD

THIS QUOTATION IS FROM STAVE _____.

THE WORDS BELONG TO _____

_____.

ONE LITERARY TECHNIQUE USED IS

_____.

ANOTHER LITERARY TECHNIQUE USED IS

_____.

THE WORD CLASS OF THE KEY WORD

" _____ " IS _____.

WRITE THE QUOTATION HERE — MAKE SURE IT IS EXACTLY THE SAME AS IT IS ON THE OTHER SIDE!

ASK: HOW DOES THIS MAKE YOU FEEL?

ASK: WOULD VICTORIANS HAVE FELT THE SAME?

ASK: HOW DOES THIS LINK TO CONTEXT?

ASK: DO OTHER QUOTATIONS LINK TO THIS?

STAVE FIVE TIMELINE

Scrooge is back at home.

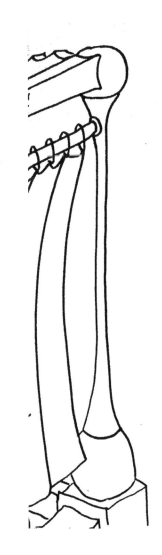

"Yes!

and the
bedpost
was his
own."

FLASHCARD

THIS QUOTATION IS FROM STAVE _____.

THE WORDS BELONG TO _____

_____.

ONE LITERARY TECHNIQUE USED IS

_____.

ANOTHER LITERARY TECHNIQUE USED IS

_____.

THE WORD CLASS OF THE KEY WORD

" _____ " IS _____.

WRITE THE QUOTATION HERE — MAKE SURE IT IS EXACTLY THE SAME AS IT IS ON THE OTHER SIDE!

ASK: HOW DOES THIS MAKE YOU FEEL?

ASK: WOULD VICTORIANS HAVE FELT THE SAME?

ASK: HOW DOES THIS LINK TO CONTEXT?

ASK: DO OTHER QUOTATIONS LINK TO THIS?

"He was so fluttered and so glowing in his good intentions, that his broken voice would scarcely answer to his call."

FLASHCARD

TEAR THIS PAGE OUT, FILL THIS SIDE IN AND BINGO! YOU HAVE A FABULOUS FLASHCARD.

THIS QUOTATION IS FROM STAVE _____.

THE WORDS BELONG TO _____

_____.

ONE LITERARY TECHNIQUE USED IS

_____.

ANOTHER LITERARY TECHNIQUE USED IS

_____.

THE WORD CLASS OF THE KEY WORD

" _____ " IS _____.

WRITE THE QUOTATION HERE — MAKE SURE IT IS <u>EXACTLY</u> THE SAME AS IT IS ON THE OTHER SIDE!

ASK: HOW DOES THIS MAKE YOU FEEL?
ASK: WOULD VICTORIANS HAVE FELT THE SAME?
ASK: HOW DOES THIS LINK TO CONTEXT?
ASK: DO OTHER QUOTATIONS LINK TO THIS?

"I am as light as a feather, I am as happy as an angel, I am as merry as a schoolboy, I am as giddy as a drunken man."

FLASHCARD

TEAR THIS PAGE OUT, FILL THIS SIDE IN AND BINGO! YOU HAVE A FABULOUS FLASHCARD.

THIS QUOTATION IS FROM STAVE _____.

THE WORDS BELONG TO _____

_____.

ONE LITERARY TECHNIQUE USED IS

_____.

ANOTHER LITERARY TECHNIQUE USED IS

_____.

THE WORD CLASS OF THE KEY WORD

" _____ " IS _____.

WRITE THE QUOTATION HERE — MAKE SURE IT IS EXACTLY THE SAME AS IT IS ON THE OTHER SIDE!

ASK: HOW DOES THIS MAKE YOU FEEL?

ASK: WOULD VICTORIANS HAVE FELT THE SAME?

ASK: HOW DOES THIS LINK TO CONTEXT?

ASK: DO OTHER QUOTATIONS LINK TO THIS?

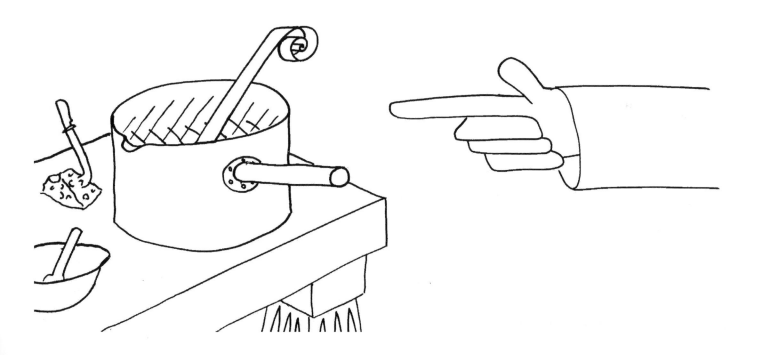

FLASHCARD

TEAR THIS PAGE OUT, FILL THIS SIDE IN AND BINGO! YOU HAVE A FABULOUS FLASHCARD.

THIS QUOTATION IS FROM STAVE _____.

THE WORDS BELONG TO _____

_____

ONE LITERARY TECHNIQUE USED IS

_____

ANOTHER LITERARY TECHNIQUE USED IS

_____

THE WORD CLASS OF THE KEY WORD

" _____ " IS _____.

WRITE THE QUOTATION HERE — MAKE SURE IT IS <u>EXACTLY</u> THE SAME AS IT IS ON THE OTHER SIDE!

ASK: HOW DOES THIS MAKE YOU FEEL?

ASK: WOULD VICTORIANS HAVE FELT THE SAME?

ASK: HOW DOES THIS LINK TO CONTEXT?

ASK: DO OTHER QUOTATIONS LINK TO THIS?

"I'm quite a baby."

FLASHCARD

TEAR THIS PAGE OUT, FILL THIS SIDE IN AND BINGO! YOU HAVE A FABULOUS FLASHCARD.

THIS QUOTATION IS FROM STAVE _____.

THE WORDS BELONG TO _____

_____.

ONE LITERARY TECHNIQUE USED IS

_____.

ANOTHER LITERARY TECHNIQUE USED IS

_____.

THE WORD CLASS OF THE KEY WORD

" _____ " IS _____.

WRITE THE QUOTATION HERE — MAKE SURE IT IS EXACTLY THE SAME AS IT IS ON THE OTHER SIDE!

ASK: HOW DOES THIS MAKE YOU FEEL?
ASK: WOULD VICTORIANS HAVE FELT THE SAME?
ASK: HOW DOES THIS LINK TO CONTEXT?
ASK: DO OTHER QUOTATIONS LINK TO THIS?

"Golden sunlight;
heavenly sky;
Sweet fresh air;
merry bells.
Oh, glorious!
Glorious!"

FLASHCARD

TEAR THIS PAGE OUT, FILL THIS SIDE IN AND BINGO! YOU HAVE A FABULOUS FLASHCARD.

THIS QUOTATION IS FROM STAVE _____ .

THE WORDS BELONG TO _____

_____ .

ONE LITERARY TECHNIQUE USED IS

_____

_____ .

ANOTHER LITERARY TECHNIQUE USED IS

_____

_____

THE WORD CLASS OF THE KEY WORD

" _____ " IS

_____ _____ .

WRITE THE QUOTATION HERE — MAKE SURE IT IS EXACTLY THE SAME AS IT IS ON THE OTHER SIDE!

ASK: HOW DOES THIS MAKE YOU FEEL?

ASK: WOULD VICTORIANS HAVE FELT THE SAME?

ASK: HOW DOES THIS LINK TO CONTEXT?

ASK: DO OTHER QUOTATIONS LINK TO THIS?

"The Spirits have done it all in one night. They can do anything they like. Of course they can. Of course they can."

FLASHCARD

TEAR THIS PAGE OUT, FILL THIS SIDE IN AND BINGO! YOU HAVE A FABULOUS FLASHCARD.

THIS QUOTATION IS FROM STAVE _____.

THE WORDS BELONG TO _____

_____.

ONE LITERARY TECHNIQUE USED IS

_____.

ANOTHER LITERARY TECHNIQUE USED IS

_____.

THE WORD CLASS OF THE KEY WORD

" _____ " IS _____.

WRITE THE QUOTATION HERE — MAKE SURE IT IS EXACTLY THE SAME AS IT IS ON THE OTHER SIDE!

ASK: HOW DOES THIS MAKE YOU FEEL?

ASK: WOULD VICTORIANS HAVE FELT THE SAME?

ASK: HOW DOES THIS LINK TO CONTEXT?

ASK: DO OTHER QUOTATIONS LINK TO THIS?

"Not the little prize turkey."

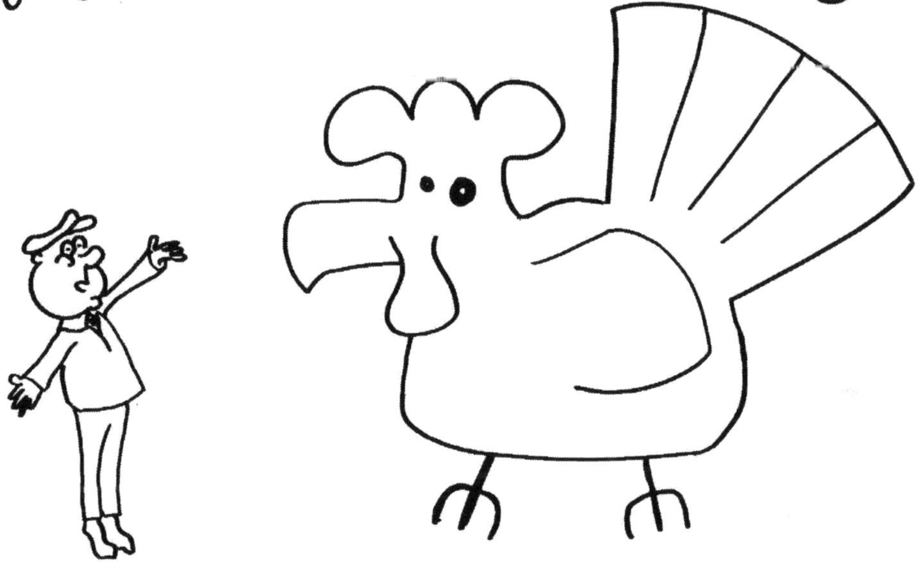

"What! The one as big as me?"

FLASHCARD

TEAR THIS PAGE OUT, FILL THIS SIDE IN AND BINGO! YOU HAVE A FABULOUS FLASHCARD.

THIS QUOTATION IS FROM STAVE _____ .

THE WORDS BELONG TO _____

_____ .

ONE LITERARY TECHNIQUE USED IS

_____ .

ANOTHER LITERARY TECHNIQUE USED IS

_____ .

THE WORD CLASS OF THE KEY WORD

" _____ " IS _____ .

WRITE THE QUOTATION HERE — MAKE SURE IT IS EXACTLY THE SAME AS IT IS ON THE OTHER SIDE!

ASK: HOW DOES THIS MAKE YOU FEEL?

ASK: WOULD VICTORIANS HAVE FELT THE SAME?

ASK: HOW DOES THIS LINK TO CONTEXT?

ASK: DO OTHER QUOTATIONS LINK TO THIS?

FLASHCARD

TEAR THIS PAGE OUT, FILL THIS SIDE IN AND BINGO! YOU HAVE A FABULOUS FLASHCARD.

THIS QUOTATION IS FROM STAVE _____ .

THE WORDS BELONG TO _____

_____ .

ONE LITERARY TECHNIQUE USED IS

_____ .

ANOTHER LITERARY TECHNIQUE USED IS

_____ .

THE WORD CLASS OF THE KEY WORD

" _____ " IS _____ .

WRITE THE QUOTATION HERE — MAKE SURE IT IS <u>EXACTLY</u> THE SAME AS IT IS ON THE <u>OTHER</u> SIDE!

ASK: HOW DOES THIS MAKE YOU FEEL?

ASK: WOULD VICTORIANS HAVE FELT THE SAME?

ASK: HOW DOES THIS LINK TO CONTEXT?

ASK: DO OTHER QUOTATIONS LINK TO THIS?

"'If you please,' said Scrooge. 'Not a farthing less. A great many back-payments are included in it, I assure you.'"

FLASHCARD

TEAR THIS PAGE OUT, FILL THIS SIDE IN AND BINGO! YOU HAVE A FABULOUS FLASHCARD.

THIS QUOTATION IS FROM STAVE _____.

THE WORDS BELONG TO _____

_____.

ONE LITERARY TECHNIQUE USED IS

_____.

ANOTHER LITERARY TECHNIQUE USED IS

_____.

THE WORD CLASS OF THE KEY WORD

" _____ " IS _____.

WRITE THE QUOTATION HERE — MAKE SURE IT IS EXACTLY THE SAME AS IT IS ON THE OTHER SIDE!

ASK: HOW DOES THIS MAKE YOU FEEL?

ASK: WOULD VICTORIANS HAVE FELT THE SAME?

ASK: HOW DOES THIS LINK TO CONTEXT?

ASK: DO OTHER QUOTATIONS LINK TO THIS?

FLASHCARD

TEAR THIS PAGE OUT, FILL THIS SIDE IN AND BINGO! YOU HAVE A FABULOUS FLASHCARD.

THIS QUOTATION IS FROM STAVE _____ .

THE WORDS BELONG TO _____

_____ .

ONE LITERARY TECHNIQUE USED IS

_____ .

ANOTHER LITERARY TECHNIQUE USED IS

_____

THE WORD CLASS OF THE KEY WORD

" _____ " IS

_____ _____ .

WRITE THE QUOTATION HERE — MAKE SURE IT IS <u>EXACTLY</u> THE SAME AS IT IS ON THE OTHER SIDE!

ASK: HOW DOES THIS MAKE YOU FEEL?

ASK: WOULD VICTORIANS HAVE FELT THE SAME?

ASK: HOW DOES THIS LINK TO CONTEXT?

ASK: DO OTHER QUOTATIONS LINK TO THIS?

"The clock struck nine. No Bob. A quarter past. No Bob. He was a full eighteen minutes and a half behind his time."

FLASHCARD

TEAR THIS PAGE OUT, FILL THIS SIDE IN AND BINGO! YOU HAVE A FABULOUS FLASHCARD.

THIS QUOTATION IS FROM STAVE _____ .

THE WORDS BELONG TO _____

_____ .

ONE LITERARY TECHNIQUE USED IS

_____ .

ANOTHER LITERARY TECHNIQUE USED IS

_____ .

THE WORD CLASS OF THE KEY WORD

" _____ " IS _____ .

WRITE THE QUOTATION HERE — MAKE SURE IT IS EXACTLY THE SAME AS IT IS ON THE OTHER SIDE !

ASK: HOW DOES THIS MAKE YOU FEEL?

ASK: WOULD VICTORIANS HAVE FELT THE SAME?

ASK: HOW DOES THIS LINK TO CONTEXT?

ASK: DO OTHER QUOTATIONS LINK TO THIS?

FLASHCARD

TEAR THIS PAGE OUT, FILL THIS SIDE IN AND BINGO! YOU HAVE A FABULOUS FLASHCARD.

THIS QUOTATION IS FROM STAVE _____.

THE WORDS BELONG TO _____

_____.

ONE LITERARY TECHNIQUE USED IS

_____.

ANOTHER LITERARY TECHNIQUE USED IS

_____.

THE WORD CLASS OF THE KEY WORD

" _____ " IS _____.

WRITE THE QUOTATION HERE — MAKE SURE IT IS EXACTLY THE SAME AS IT IS ON THE OTHER SIDE!

ASK: HOW DOES THIS MAKE YOU FEEL?

ASK: WOULD VICTORIANS HAVE FELT THE SAME?

ASK: HOW DOES THIS LINK TO CONTEXT?

ASK: DO OTHER QUOTATIONS LINK TO THIS?

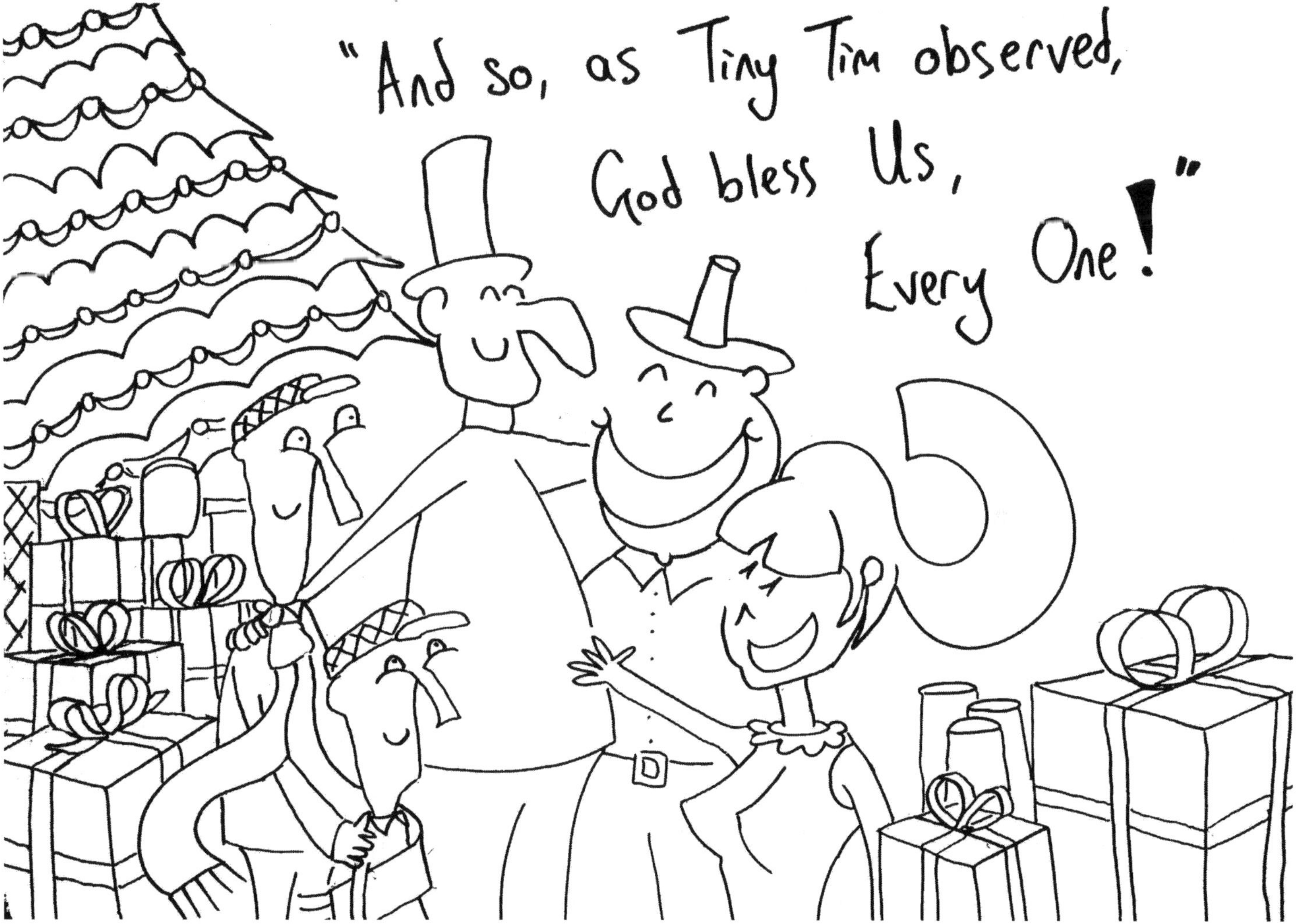
"And so, as Tiny Tim observed,
God bless Us,
Every One!"

FLASHCARD

TEAR THIS PAGE OUT, FILL THIS SIDE IN AND BINGO! YOU HAVE A FABULOUS FLASHCARD.

THIS QUOTATION IS FROM STAVE _____.

THE WORDS BELONG TO _____

_____.

ONE LITERARY TECHNIQUE USED IS

_____.

ANOTHER LITERARY TECHNIQUE USED IS

_____.

THE WORD CLASS OF THE KEY WORD

" _____ " IS _____.

WRITE THE QUOTATION HERE — MAKE SURE IT IS <u>EXACTLY</u> THE SAME AS IT IS ON THE OTHER SIDE!

ASK: HOW DOES THIS MAKE YOU FEEL?

ASK: WOULD VICTORIANS HAVE FELT THE SAME?

ASK: HOW DOES THIS LINK TO CONTEXT?

ASK: DO OTHER QUOTATIONS LINK TO THIS?

AND
NOW...

Don't forget to photograph and share your doodles with your friends— they need the quotations too!

(Wear your best baseball hat and flares, obv.)

Pick your own quotation...

...and do a doodle to suit it.

FLASHCARD

TEAR THIS PAGE OUT, FILL THIS SIDE IN AND BINGO! YOU HAVE A FABULOUS FLASHCARD.

THIS QUOTATION IS FROM STAVE _____.

THE WORDS BELONG TO _____

_____.

ONE LITERARY TECHNIQUE USED IS

_____.

ANOTHER LITERARY TECHNIQUE USED IS

_____.

THE WORD CLASS OF THE KEY WORD

" _____ " IS _____.

WRITE THE QUOTATION HERE — MAKE SURE IT IS EXACTLY THE SAME AS IT IS ON THE OTHER SIDE!

ASK: HOW DOES THIS MAKE YOU FEEL?
ASK: WOULD VICTORIANS HAVE FELT THE SAME?
ASK: HOW DOES THIS LINK TO CONTEXT?
ASK: DO OTHER QUOTATIONS LINK TO THIS?

Pick your own quotation...

...and do a doodle to suit it.

FLASHCARD

TEAR THIS PAGE OUT, FILL THIS SIDE IN AND BINGO! YOU HAVE A FABULOUS FLASHCARD.

THIS QUOTATION IS FROM STAVE _____.

THE WORDS BELONG TO _____

_____.

ONE LITERARY TECHNIQUE USED IS

_____.

ANOTHER LITERARY TECHNIQUE USED IS

_____.

THE WORD CLASS OF THE KEY WORD

" _____ " IS _____.

WRITE THE QUOTATION HERE — MAKE SURE IT IS EXACTLY THE SAME AS IT IS ON THE OTHER SIDE!

ASK: HOW DOES THIS MAKE YOU FEEL?
ASK: WOULD VICTORIANS HAVE FELT THE SAME?
ASK: HOW DOES THIS LINK TO CONTEXT?
ASK: DO OTHER QUOTATIONS LINK TO THIS?

Pick your own quotation...

...and do a doodle to suit it.

FLASHCARD

TEAR THIS PAGE OUT, FILL THIS SIDE IN AND BINGO! YOU HAVE A FABULOUS FLASHCARD.

THIS QUOTATION IS FROM STAVE _____ .

THE WORDS BELONG TO _____

_____ .

ONE LITERARY TECHNIQUE USED IS

_____ .

ANOTHER LITERARY TECHNIQUE USED IS

_____ .

THE WORD CLASS OF THE KEY WORD

" _____ " IS _____ .

WRITE THE QUOTATION HERE — MAKE SURE IT IS EXACTLY THE SAME AS IT IS ON THE OTHER SIDE!

ASK: HOW DOES THIS MAKE YOU FEEL?

ASK: WOULD VICTORIANS HAVE FELT THE SAME?

ASK: HOW DOES THIS LINK TO CONTEXT?

ASK: DO OTHER QUOTATIONS LINK TO THIS?

Pick your own quotation...

...and do a doodle to suit it.

FLASHCARD

TEAR THIS PAGE OUT, FILL THIS SIDE IN AND BINGO! YOU HAVE A FABULOUS FLASHCARD.

THIS QUOTATION IS FROM STAVE _____ .

THE WORDS BELONG TO _____

_____ .

ONE LITERARY TECHNIQUE USED IS

_____ .

ANOTHER LITERARY TECHNIQUE USED IS

_____ .

THE WORD CLASS OF THE KEY WORD

" _____ " IS _____ .

WRITE THE QUOTATION HERE — MAKE SURE IT IS EXACTLY THE SAME AS IT IS ON THE OTHER SIDE!

ASK: HOW DOES THIS MAKE YOU FEEL?

ASK: WOULD VICTORIANS HAVE FELT THE SAME?

ASK: HOW DOES THIS LINK TO CONTEXT?

ASK: DO OTHER QUOTATIONS LINK TO THIS?

Pick your own quotation...

...and do a doodle to suit it.

FLASHCARD

TEAR THIS PAGE OUT, FILL THIS SIDE IN AND BINGO! YOU HAVE A FABULOUS FLASHCARD.

THIS QUOTATION IS FROM STAVE _____.

THE WORDS BELONG TO _____

_____.

ONE LITERARY TECHNIQUE USED IS

_____.

ANOTHER LITERARY TECHNIQUE USED IS

_____.

THE WORD CLASS OF THE KEY WORD

" _____ " IS _____.

WRITE THE QUOTATION HERE — MAKE SURE IT IS EXACTLY THE SAME AS IT IS ON THE OTHER SIDE!

ASK: HOW DOES THIS MAKE YOU FEEL?
ASK: WOULD VICTORIANS HAVE FELT THE SAME?
ASK: HOW DOES THIS LINK TO CONTEXT?
ASK: DO OTHER QUOTATIONS LINK TO THIS?

OF COURSE, NONE OF THIS IS ANY SORT OF SUBSTITUTE FOR ACTUALLY READING THE BOOK ➡

(The crocodile attack scene is especially thrilling.)

Printed in Poland
by Amazon Fulfillment
Poland Sp. z o.o., Wrocław